MEN IN SEARCH OF WORK

AND THE WOMEN WHO LOVE THEM

DIANE EBLE

MEN IN SEARCH OF WORK

AND THE WOMEN WHO LOVE THEM

ZondervanPublishingHouse
Grand Rapids, Michigan

A Division of HarperCollinsPublishers

Men in Search of Work and the Women Who Love Them
Copyright © 1994 by Diane Eble

Requests for information should be addressed to:
Zondervan Publishing House
Grand Rapids, Michigan 49530

Library of Congress Cataloging-in-Publication Data

Eble, Diane
    Men in search of work and the women who love them / Diane
Eble
        p. cm.
    Includes bibliographical references and index.
    ISBN 0-310-39721-9 (softcover)
    1. Unemployed—Religious life. 2. Unemployed—Family
relationships. 3. Unemployed—Life skills guides. 4.
Job hunting—Religious aspects—Christianity. 5. Church
work with the employed. 6. Family—Religious life. 7.
Unemployed—United States.
I. Title.
BV4596.U53
248.8′8—dc20   93-35822
                                                         CIP

Edited by Linda Vanderzalm
Cover design by Rick Devon

Printed in the United States of America

94 95 96 97 98 / DH / 10 9 8 7 6 5 4 3 2 1

To all those who shared their stories,
courageously,
candidly,
and to everyone who cares enough to reach out

• Contents •

• Acknowledgments •

Writing a book like this one, like searching for a job, is a wonderful exercise in interdependence. I needed my network of friends, co-workers, and acquaintances to contact people who would share their stories and expertise. Thank you to all who had a part in that process.

I'm most grateful for the courageous people who were willing to be interviewed. This book would not offer the breadth and depth it does without your stories. You were incredibly open about your deepest griefs and wounds, and your stories are, I believe, what will give others hope.

Special thanks to Vic and Betsey Glavach, who were willing to be named, and to Gregg Lewis for his article that interviewed the Glavaches for *Marriage Partnership*. You articulated so well the experience of career trauma and how it affected your lives.

Thanks also to the many people who lent their expertise to this project: Dr. Ronald Jensen and Dr. Ken Potts, for their psychological insights; Rick Ehlers, Ron Moskal, David Bates, Karen Volpert, Joy Maguire Dooley, Lloyd Bach, Maureen Rodgers, and Jan Barber for their help and suggestions about support groups.

Thank you to Walt Meloon and the other staff members of Turnaround ministries for inviting me to the "Turnaround Blizzard" Weekend and to those who shared their stories there. Hearing how you have gone through the fire yet found

God faithful bolstered my own faith and confidence that with God's help no crisis is too great for us to handle.

Thank you to Sarah Guthrie, who linked me to valuable research. Thanks to Charlene Baumbich, who became a magnet for attracting just the right information at just the right time and who was a constant encouragement.

Some of the information in appendix A is adapted from Richard Hagstrom's Green Light Concept. I am grateful to him and to others such as Richard Bolles, Arthur Miller, and Ralph Mattson, who have helped me to define my life purpose and help others discover their "motivated apititudes and skills."

Finally, a heartfelt thanks to Gene, my husband, the most courageous person of all for allowing me to share some of our painful struggles. Without you, this book would not have been written. Without your support, this book could not have been written.

• Introduction •

To tell you the truth, I didn't want to write this book. Living through my husband's employment struggles was not something I enjoyed, and I did not relish rehashing it in a book. It would have been much easier to put the whole experience behind me and move on.

But even as I tried to do that, I kept bumping into other people who were experiencing the pain, isolation, and confusion that I attempted to put behind me. I picked up the newspapers and read nearly every day how major companies were laying off thousands of people. And it was as if I sensed the pain multiplying all around me, like so many fast-growing cancerous tumors. I began to talk to people who had been laid off. People who, like the airline pilot for a now-defunct airline, were trying to deal with the loss of a career they loved and the prospect of having to start all over in some field that lurked behind a dark cloud. Behind all the statistics of layoffs were real people who were trying to cope with loss of self-esteem, loss of income, a sudden cutting off of social relationships, and often even a radical rethinking of their basic views of reality. (How could this happen? Why did this happen to me? Do I have the resources to cope?)

Beyond the numbers of those actually laid off, I knew there were many, many others holding on to their job, but wondering for how long. And if I'm to believe the career counselors I know and read, as many as four out of five people who do have jobs do not enjoy their work. Maybe in recession-wracked days they try to drum up enough gratitude for even having a job to get them through each day, but secretly they wonder if it's worth it. Others put food on the table by piecing together several part-time jobs. Still other men struggle to find a satisfying career niche, for any number of reasons, ranging from personal problems to where they happen to live. They may be underemployed, keenly aware they are not using their education or talents to the fullest. Finally, some have silently slipped into the ranks of the "discouraged worker"—able-bodied people who have just given up on looking for work.

The discouraged worker, the dissatisfied worker, the underemployed—none of these people is figured into the unemployment statistics. If ten million people are unemployed at any given time, probably tens of millions are facing a job crisis besides unemployment. They are being forced to rethink their view of work—what it means, what to expect from it, how to make it enjoyable.

I heard the silent cries of those struggling with a job crisis because my ears were already attuned to that particular language of pain. At the same time, I noticed that many could not articulate their distress and that too often their friends and relatives who wanted to help had no idea just how to reach out. I began to feel somehow that I could not, should not, go on my way without giving expression to the problem.

So I wrote an article for a Christian magazine. I wrote it under a pseudonym, to protect my husband and myself from the embarrassment that is associated with not fitting the cultural norm of having a successful career. I interviewed other couples who faced unemployment. I talked with men who hadn't found their niche in life and with men who had a good job but then had been laid off and were having trouble finding another job. I listened to men who were successful and thought they had it made financially until they suddenly found themselves the victim of the "downsizing" and mergers that have begun to characterize the business climate of the last several years.

I interviewed fourteen couples and twelve individuals in depth; some of the stories I've followed over a period of four years. At a retreat with Turnaround Ministries, I listened to the stories of fourteen other couples who were facing bankruptcy or other severe business setbacks.

As I listened, I noticed something. Everyone found the interviews to be a positive experience. Couples said things to me, in front of each other, that they somehow could not tell each other. They gave voice to the pain and frustration—and the new perspectives and insights that led to a growth they would not have chosen but now would not trade. And they found relief. They were not alone, and they were not "strange" for the way they felt. Some of them discovered new depths in their own character, their relationship to their spouse and to God. Communicating the experience led to relief. Later, after the article was published, I found that reading about the experience gave other people the same relief: "I'm not alone. Others have felt these feelings to some degree. Others have grown through this. So can I."

Those are the twin messages of this book. "You are not alone: others have experienced something of what you now feel." And, "Those who have gone through this and have come out on the other side have found the experience has not destroyed them. Rather, they have grown."

How to Use This Book

If you're reading this book, it's either because you're undergoing a career crisis yourself, or your spouse is experiencing the crisis and you are concerned and deeply affected yourself. This book will help you understand the dynamics of a career crisis and some of the better ways to weather this storm.

I concentrated on men and the effect of an unsatisfying (or nonexistent) career because, despite the cultural changes regarding gender of the past two decades, work is central to the identity of most men. Indeed, a recent study by the consumer- and social-research firm Yankelovich Partners, Inc., found that 63 percent of men feel that being the primary wage-earner is what makes them feel most manly. For their part, 88 percent of the women said they want to feel protected by the men in their lives—which includes the protection of financial provision, if I'm to believe other studies and the people I interviewed.[1] The book concentrates on the unique aspects of being a male without satisfying work and of being married to a man who is without satisfying work.

But I did not want merely to describe the experience of facing career trauma. This is also a book of hope and encouragement and practical application: people will share what has helped them, not just their perspective but also the practical things they did for themselves and the practical ways others reached out to lessen the burden. The book explores a variety of resources—practical, spiritual, community, and church-based.

I've prepared some discussion questions to help you integrate some of the ideas in the chapters. You may want to answer these questions in a personal journal, or you may find it helpful to discuss the questions together with your spouse. Some of you may want to meet with other couples going through a job crisis and use the questions as a guide for group discussion.

I intentionally lean more on experience than science or Scripture, on questions rather than answers. It was only after Job exhausted himself through questioning that he was able to hear and see God.

A career crisis has a way of forcing many other issues to the forefront. It tends to throw a floodlight on unconscious expectations: that family and/or church will be there when you need them; that your corporation or your Christian employer is supposed to take care of you. For my own part, Gene's career crisis made me question why I married someone whose career path was not fixed. My questions led to some surprising and painful answers and made me confront some old issues I had tried to bury.

Theological questions also came up for me and others. Is God really in control of our lives? Why did he let this happen? Why is this situation continuing, despite our best efforts? Does this life offer us any kind of future, or should we just put all our hope in heaven? How does God answer prayer? How should I pray? Should I pray for a specific job or just that God would provide for my needs? Am I really trusting God, or am I trusting in the security a job brings?

All of these are painful questions to confront. Some people do not confront them. They find ways not to feel bad—alcohol, drugs, pleasure, lust, materialism, whatever. Other people simply concentrate their efforts on finding a new job—fast. Indeed, this is the advice of all the books I've read. "Sure, job loss is traumatic. But you have to get over the emotions and move on. Otherwise it will hamper your job search."

And of course, the advice is solid, to an extent: if you're unemployed, that is the immediate crisis, and the obvious answer is to find another job. But if you find yourself in a job crisis, don't squelch the feelings, doubts, and questions that plague you after the two hundredth résumé has been filed and the last contact has promised to get in touch if he or she hears of a job opening. I invite you to tune in to your feelings, open this book, and turn to whatever section deals with the matter that concerns you at the moment. Journey with me and the other people whose stories you will hear candidly told. Let your questions rise to the surface, and tune your heart to God giving you some answers.

People who bring their pain to God will first feel the pain. Look at the Bible; look at the Psalms. Godly people don't run away from their pain.

The only way out of the pain is through it. As you read the experiences of others, you may find similar feelings welling up inside yourself. Don't fight it. Go through it; I promise you, you will emerge. And when you do, the feelings will be behind you. Oh, you may have to revisit them again. But it will be more like stepping gingerly through a puddle rather than that first-time experience of wading through knee-deep mud.

As you work through this process—and never forget, it is a process—you will begin to sense a purpose for your present experience. And this sense of purpose may lead to a very strange thing: joy. The kind of joy James is talking about when he says, "Consider it pure joy [pure joy!], my brothers, whenever you face trials of many kinds [unemployment certainly involves this], because you know that the testing of your faith develops perseverance. Perseverance must finish its work so that you may be mature and complete, not lacking anything" (James 1:2–4).

• Part I •

Career Crisis
from the Inside

· 1 ·

Expectations and Losses

For years, my husband, Gene, and I dreaded what we thought of as *The Question:* "So, Gene, what do you do for a living?"

What Gene did for a living in those days was work odd jobs—sales mostly—while trying to break into advertising. He knocked on a lot of doors, built up a portfolio, even went back to school and earned a master's degree. While every other man we knew was steadily climbing a career ladder (or so it seemed), Gene was still trying to find the ladder. Because our society socializes men from birth to define their self-identity through work and career, Gene found it hard to admit his struggle.

So in response to *The Question,* we gave a sugar-coated answer, trying to make our situation palatable to those around us, all of whom seemed to be charging toward the American Dream while we trailed behind in the dust.

We felt alone. We hid behind a smoke screen ("Everything's fine," we kept saying) and tried to cope with the severe tensions placed on us individually and as a couple because of Gene's lack of a steady and fulfilling job.

Now I know we're not alone. In these days of recession, downsizing, mergers, and fast-paced technology that renders not only positions but whole jobs obsolete, countless people face employment problems of all kinds. Take Richard Wheat, a hospital administrator, who lost his job due to a "reorganization." In his early fifties, Richard has been looking for a job for three years. Most employers tell him he's overqualified.

Then there's Michael Catlin, who worked for a bank for two years until new management decided to reorganize. He then found work as a management trainee, but when he wouldn't be a part of questionable ethical practices, the bank terminated his job. His first period of unemployment lasted nine months, the second two-and-a-half years. Meanwhile, his wife, Martha, found a job she loved. Coping with forced role reversal brought on what they call a "psychological, social, and spiritual low in our marriage."

Not having satisfying work affects every aspect of a man's life. It reaches its fingers of pain into every relationship, including his relationship with himself, his spouse, his family, his peers, his church, and his God.

The pain within himself may be the deepest. A man may feel as if he's failed to live up to expectations—his own, his family's, his culture's, perhaps even God's.

GREAT EXPECTATIONS

Men keenly feel the pressure to live up to the cultural definition of success. Americans have come to worship career status as a measure of worth, suggests futurist Selwyn Enzer. Our culture defines success not only as having a good job but also as moving along a career, making a significant contribution, and of course, earning more and more money in the process. The pressure to succeed may come from without, especially if the man's family embraces it and his community reflects it. Or the pressure can come from within, from the expectations a man has set for himself.

Many men add yet another element to their work expectations: satisfaction. "Men still see themselves as providers," Michael Catlin told me. "We also want to be fulfilled in our jobs." Many of the men I talked to were in the baby-boomer generation, and they told of fathers who hated their jobs but did them because they felt they had no choice. The sons, observing this, vowed things would be different for them. They would get an education and find a good job that provided not only for their material needs but also for their psychological and spiritual needs. A whole generation upped the ante for what spells career success. Not only did they have to fulfill the American myth that each generation must better its living standard in order to be successful, they also had to have a job that gave them satisfaction and fulfillment.

A man who doesn't fit the mold, who doesn't measure up to his own or his culture's idea of career success, will feel like a failure. Whether he has not yet found a satisfying career niche or he is unemployed, he will feel as if he is on the outside.

Brett Parrish holds two master's degrees and is ordained in a large Protestant denomination. After he graduated from seminary, he worked a series of "odd, non-career jobs" to support his growing family. Then he found a good job with a Christian organization and moved his family to the Midwest. A year later, he lost his job and returned to working several part-time jobs plus doing free-lance work while he prepared himself for the pastorate.

Parrish was very bothered by the fact that his life is not conforming to the accepted norms for a man's career. "Both my father and my wife's father worked for the same firm all their lives," he said. "Their careers followed a logical progression. What has concerned me most about my present situation is not the financial aspects but that here I am, thirty-nine and without a career. If I'm not established in a career by now, I wonder if I'll ever be. I would like to be established, not dabbling. A job is so critical to a man's identity. I feel I haven't made any progress in the normal career path a man is supposed to have."

His last words struck me. I suspect all men have this picture of "the normal career path a man is supposed to have" in their minds, and they measure themselves against this. If they don't measure up, they feel inferior. My husband, Gene, told me, "In our culture, a job is the most important thing a man has. I may not agree with that, but the idea still kicks around my soul somewhere." Perhaps it "kicks around his soul somewhere" because it touches on something deep within the masculine soul. Dr. Larry Crabb, author of *Men & Women*, believes this is so. He believes that men have a deep passion to know they can do something well, to move purposefully through life aware that what they have to give makes a difference. When that passion is frustrated, a man is out of sync with his very being. Gene said, "I felt I wasn't doing my share, and that led to stress." He called it stress, and certainly it was that. But knowing him well, I would call it something even more painful: shame.

VOCATIONALLY NAKED

Shame is a particularly debilitating emotion. When shame is operating, it cancels out the energy we need to get back on our feet. As Gershen Kaufman, author of *The Psychology of Shame,* points out, all of us must have a dream, an inner vision that directs our path, pulling us toward it, shaping itself into being through imagination. The guiding dream can take any form; it is a mental picture that defines our purpose in life. We construct our lives around our dream, but when something—like job crisis—thwarts our dream, we feel a sense of powerlessness and shame. "Shame becomes activated whenever . . . fundamental expectations of self (imagined scenes of accomplishment or purpose) are suddenly exposed as wrong or are thwarted."[1] Unless we get over the shame and reclaim the dream, we will lose that sense of purpose.

Men have described just this sense of disorientation and purposelessness. "When you're fired from your job, you look the same, breathe the same air, and still bleed when you're cut. But, imperceptibly, a metamorphosis takes place. You cross over into the world of the unemployed, a world where there seems to be no other occupants. There really are others, but they are silent and invisible, fighting their growing feelings of shame and worthlessness. They have been rejected, and no one appears to desire what they have to offer."[2]

Warren Farrell, a leading spokesperson for the current men's movement, likens being fired to rape: "Rape feels to women like being fired feels to men." Women may find his statement offensive. But what he is trying to communicate is that being fired is, to most men, about the worst thing they can imagine happening to them. It does violence to the very soul of a man.

Farrell's analogy contains other parallels. Losing a job leaves a man feeling victimized by powerful forces outside himself. He feels his sense of control, of power over his environment has been wrenched away. He feels robbed, stripped of his identity. His view that the world worked in a certain way and that he could maneuver his way through that world is shattered. He is vocationally naked.

And he feels the shame.

CAUGHT IN A DOWNWARD SPIRAL

Some men get mired in this sense of shame. One couple I interviewed in depth four years ago was clearly in trouble. The husband could not let anyone else know of his true situation (he had left his job in retail to work with a new business and for two years did not earn any money at that endeavor). His marriage suffered and eventually has deteriorated to the point where, the last I talked to his wife, he is trying to divorce her. Even though he was successful in one job for three years after that traumatic period, he said he still saw himself as a failure.

"The other day I saw a man who used to know me when I was struggling," Derek Halstad told me. "I said, 'You have my address.' He said jokingly, 'Yeah, but should I have it in the temporary or permanent file?' I resented that attitude of 'What job are you doing now?' I've always been willing to work. But if you don't drop down into the groove like everyone else, you get to feeling as if there's something wrong with you. It's hard to fight that when your résumé looks like Swiss cheese. I still feel as if I'm not much in the eyes of anyone else."

This sense of being "not much in the eyes of everyone else"—or in your own eyes—is the biggest danger of any job crisis. It can lead to a loss of confidence, lowered expectations (which can then become self-fulfilling prophecies), and, in the worst case, discouragement to the point of giving up altogether.

No one knows exactly how many "discouraged workers"—people who have given up looking for a job—there are in this country because they're not counted among the jobless or included in the unemployment rate. Some experts say the ranks of the discouraged include many more than the government's quarterly surveys suggest. One research company pegs the figure for males at 19 percent of the total labor market.[3] We don't know how many early retirees, how many long-term college students, how many part-time workers are really discouraged workers.

When Terry Buss, an urban studies professor at the University of Akron, looked at discouraged workers in the United States and in Youngstown, Ohio, in the late 1980s, he discovered a "fairly high number of once highly paid workers sitting home waiting for their break."[4]

Jay Sherer is a consultant with the Derson Group, a Chicago-based outplacement firm that helps people find jobs. He said he finds it hard to redirect people whose personal problems have mushroomed as they have gone months without work. "It drains away all of their energy, and they kind of lose it," he said.

But the downward spiral is not inevitable. Researchers have found that much depends on the man himself and how he responds to his job crisis. A man does not have to be shackled by shame. The first step in preventing the downward spiral is to acknowledge exactly what you've lost, understand the common emotional reactions to loss, and concentrate on counteracting the potential negative impact of each loss. The only way *out* is *through*—letting yourself feel the emotions, setting up the systems that will enable you to focus on the positive, to get on with your job search, and to keep up your morale throughout it all.

ACKNOWLEDGE THE LOSSES

Let's look at the common losses associated with a job crisis. As you read through the list, allow yourself to feel those feelings, if you haven't already. If you're reading this because your spouse has lost his job, think of times he might have felt this way or clues that hint he may be feeling this now.

Loss of Identity

As we've seen, a job crisis often involves a loss of self-esteem and sometimes even a loss of identity. We wonder what to tell people at a party when they ask *The Question:* "So, what do you do for a living?" Barry Crull, an airline pilot, said, "I usually say, 'I'm unemployed.' But people look at me as if I'm a bum. Maybe I should say I'm an unemployed airline pilot."

Underemployment can also lead to a confusion of identity and a loss of self-esteem. Though Brett Parrish was delivering newspapers in the morning and working part-time in a warehouse, he did not think of himself in terms of these jobs. He thought of himself as a pastor waiting for a call. When my husband, Gene, sold water-filtration systems while trying to break into advertising, he didn't see himself as a salesperson. Deciding how you see yourself and coming to terms with that, is a first step in coping with the fundamental loss of identity.

Loss of Office

An office typically confers status and identity. It's the place where workers get things done, a center for accomplishment. When that's gone, things change. Gone is access to all the amenities that would make a job search easier—an answered phone, a typist, a photocopy machine, or even simple supplies. Now it takes a lot of personal initiative and time to accomplish even the simplest task. Home changes its meaning too: it's no longer either the sanctuary from work or the locus of current work. Men may feel unwelcome at home, as if they are invading their wives' territory.

Loss of Connection

When men lose their jobs, they no longer feel a part of things. They walk down a busy street during morning rush hour and don't feel as if they belong anywhere. Everyone else has places to go, things to do. The person in a job crisis may begin to envy people of all businesses and trades, even people in occupations he never dreamed of pursuing. But he envies them because they are going to a place where people know them, address them by name, give them a regular paycheck, recognize their contribution, and care for them. "It's like someone springs a trap door out from under you and you're flying in space, trying to grab onto something," is how one former newspaper reporter described his job loss.[5]

Loss of Control

Along with losing an identity, an office, and connections, unemployment also means losing control. A job gives structure to a person's life, allowing the person to know what to expect in a day, in a week. Unemployment means everything is up for grabs. So much is out of control: who will or won't return your calls, where the job openings are, when your unemployment compensation will run out, how much you will owe in taxes—the list may seem endless.

Loss of Social Contacts

With the loss of a job comes the loss of the social network of colleagues and co-workers. One man who had lost his job said, "It proved to be very difficult to lose [my] job and [my] friends and [my] life as it had been. I had moved and changed jobs before in my life. But it had always been my idea, and this time it wasn't. Even though it has been five months [since the move to take a new job] I am still lonely."[6]

Not only that, men in job crisis may feel unsure of their social role. Some unemployed couples find that their friends drop them, especially if they have had to cut back financially and can no longer afford the social activities they had done together.

Loss of Income

The loss of income resulting from a job crisis can be devastating, especially if the couple doesn't have the three- to six-month "cushion" of living expenses in savings all the experts recommend. Financial problems have a way of muddying all the other issues and causing plenty of problems of their own. As we've discussed, loss of income can mean losing social contacts because money is not available to do things with friends.

Money means so many things to people: security, status, power. It interested me to find that two couples who did not have any financial worries (either because the severance package was good and they were confident the man would get a job soon, or because the couple had a substantial cushion of savings for living expenses), nevertheless experienced tensions about not generating an income. Money generally means power in our culture, whether or not we consciously embrace that. Not having money changes the balance of power in all relationships.

Loss of Faith in "The System"

Most of us believe that if we work hard, are honest, and possess skills, we will always be able to have a job. Yet many men have done all these things and yet do not have a good job.

Bob Marone always dreamed of working for the State Department. He got an undergraduate degree in political science from a good university and a master's degree from another. He took the State Department tests and looked hard for a job. Yet he never did attain his dream. He now works for his state's government, but he does accounting, something he hates. It's taken him years to accept that "The System" doesn't work the way he had been raised to believe it would. Other men I talked to lost their jobs just a few years before they would have retired, shattering their dream of receiving rewards for their years of service with one company.

The loss of faith in "The System" often has spiritual

implications as well: not only does the world not always work the way we had imagined, but sometimes God doesn't work the way we had imagined either. One man, who had been a vice-president of a Christian organization and held other responsible jobs, found himself unemployed for eighteen months. At the beginning of his search, he sent out more than 600 personalized letters to the organizations and people he knew. He made phone calls and followed up every reasonable lead. He did everything right, and yet as time passed, he saw fewer results from his effort. I also talked to three pastors who had lost their jobs. For each of them the job loss came as a profound shock. One said to me, "I'd always believed the church would take care of me. How could they treat me this way?"

Whenever we experience a loss, we need to grieve. Many books and experts advise men who have lost their jobs to jump immediately into the task of getting a new job. Yet they also acknowledge that people have to deal somehow with all the emotions of a job crisis if the job search is to be successful. One recent study found that people do better if they allow themselves a short cooling-off period before actively searching for re-employment. Although losing a job is stressful, a job search, a geographical move, or retraining is also inherently stressful. It's better to take some time to absorb the losses and gather emotional strength before tackling this new set of stresses. Chapter 10 will explore strategies to cope with the stresses of a job hunt.

Now let's focus on the emotions you are likely to feel at one time or another because of the job crisis. These emotions can either debilitate you or motivate you to a successful job search. Learning how to handle these losses constructively will enable you to deal with other issues—your relationship to your family, your spiritual issues, your social relationships, and your financial situation.

· 2 ·

Emotions of a Job Crisis

Since the Great Depression of the 1930s, many researchers have studied job loss and how it affects a person. Most of that research has focused on how it affects men. However, job crises affect not only the men themselves but also their spouses. This chapter will explore the emotional turmoil men experience as a result of a job crisis, and the next chapter will focus on the unique struggles of their wives.

DEVELOPING EMOTIONAL RESILIENCE

Some researchers describe stages people go through, typically beginning with feelings of shock, anger, and protest immediately following the job loss, then moving to a phase of optimism and active job search, and ending with pessimism, withdrawal, and passivity if the job search is unsuccessful.[1] Another model often used to understand loss is Elisabeth Kubler-Ross' five stages of grief: denial and isolation, anger, bargaining, depression, and acceptance.

The idea of stages may be misleading because it suggests a logical progression from one set of emotions to another.

Based on my research, personal experience, the perspectives of job counselors, and my interviews with people facing a job crisis, I believe that people tend to move back and forth between stages. The amount of emotional energy and time you spend in each stage will depend on a number of factors: your emotional makeup, your financial situation, your ability to trust God, how much time you had to prepare for job loss, how much support you receive from other people, how attached you were to your former job, and how you perceive your future prospects. You may pass through certain stages quickly and revisit others. At times you may feel you are taking two steps forward and one step backward. That's normal. The main thing is to acknowledge whatever you're feeling, deal with it, and know that "this too shall pass."

Emotions of Change

Shock. You will feel intense shock especially if the job loss is involuntary and unanticipated. You may have heard rumors in the company or seen other signs that you preferred to ignore. Or you may have known it was coming. Either way, the reality of the job loss will bring shock.

Relief. You may feel relief that the uncertainty is gone. You may feel relief that you can finally admit the job's negative aspects that you've pushed out of your conscious mind. In this stage you may feel optimistic. You know your own worth: you have solid skills and accomplishments. Perhaps you even turn down a couple of job offers because the salaries or benefits don't match what you left behind.

Denial. When the relief wears off and the new job doesn't materialize, you may take this backward step. You may cling to the hope that your employers will change their mind and hire you back once they see how much they really needed you. Some men skip the step of relief altogether and move right into denial, pretending to their wives and everyone else that they still have a job.

Anger. Everyone I talked to felt some degree of anger. This emotion can actually be positive; anger produces a lot of energy. But anger becomes debilitating if it is excessive, if you can't shake it and move on, if you blame and attack others with it, if you use it to burn bridges. This is one important emotion to deal with constructively. Remember, your past employer may be a future client and will almost certainly be contacted as a reference. Burned bridges can only burn you.

Guilt and inferiority. Steeped in the work ethic, surrounded by a culture that worships career status as a measure of worth, many men struggle with guilt and a sense of inferiority when they are in job crisis. You may feel you have no value if you are not productive. You may feel guilty of failing in your role as provider.

If you allow yourself to go through these feelings in a safe environment—with someone or some group that will allow you to feel the emotions without judging you or getting immobilized themselves—then you can move on to the next stages, which involve dealing with the realities.

Facing reality. You have a clear sense of your present circumstances. You begin to see clearly what needs to be done. You start to make the necessary financial and lifestyle adjustments. You feel able to tell others about your predicament, if you haven't already.

Depression and anxiety. As you face the realities, you may feel overwhelmed. You may find it difficult to be motivated and have a positive approach. You may be unable to see beyond your immediate circumstances to envision a better tomorrow. You may be very worried about finances and your future. You may find yourself swinging back and forth between the restlessness of anxiety and the listlessness of depression and apathy.

Acceptance. This stage is characterized by persistence, dedication to the job search, and resourcefulness. Your belief in yourself is restored and getting stronger. Your energy is focused on identifying and obtaining your next career position. You possess the energy and drive to develop an action plan for your job hunt. You sense your mission in life and feel more confident that you can obtain it.

Alternatively, this stage may force you to formulate a whole new perspective on your situation. This was the case for Bob Marone, who eventually came to accept that he would likely never obtain his dream of working for the State Department. Instead, he changed the way he saw his current job. He focused his identity on other areas of his life. The Bob Marone I interviewed four years ago was a very different man from the man I talked to most recently. He is now a man at peace with himself, his family, his peers, and God. Most job-search books assume that if people try hard enough, have faith, and deal with their emotional issues well, the result will always be the right job. I believe that sometimes acceptance means coming to grips with one's situation and finding some way to make peace with it, even if that doesn't mean getting the dream job.

To get to the point of acceptance, you need first to look reality squarely in the face rather than let it debilitate you. Discover if some of the following strategies can help you develop the emotional resilience to make this tough time a period of profound growth.

STRATEGIES FOR DEVELOPING EMOTIONAL RESILIENCE

No matter where you are in the stages outlined above, no matter what emotions you currently battle, you can benefit from the following steps.

Recognize Your Feelings

Recognize what you are feeling. Identify and accept all your emotions. Remind yourself often that you are not alone. Others have gone or will go through this process. Allow yourself time to reflect and regroup and settle into the job search.

Find a Confidant

Find someone in whom you can confide and to whom you can express your emotions. It may be your spouse, but often it's best to find someone else—a friend, another person who faces or has faced a job crisis, a pastor, or a therapist. Find someone who can handle you at your lowest. Do this as soon as possible so that you can counteract the negative effects of secrecy and isolation.

Deepen Your Support Systems

You will need a lot of support as you sort out the various pieces of your life as a result of a job crisis. Many of the following chapters will help you strengthen your relationships with your spouse, family members, friends, church members, and God. Chapter 12 will discuss the importance of support groups that will help you with the tasks of finding meaningful work. Consciously make efforts to inform people of what you are going through and what you need from them. Don't assume people know either what you are feeling or how they can help.

Overcome the Shame

Shame more than anything else can get you stuck. It's not connected to any particular stage of job crisis but can pervade the whole experience. If you struggle with shame, I suggest the following:

Acknowledge your feelings of shame to one other person. Something about acknowledging shame automatically lessens it, because shame is connected to secrecy. When you bring into the light your feeling of unworthiness, it often feels less intense. It also helps if a person who believes in you can accept your feelings and gently point out the value he or she sees in you.

If your sense of shame persists, talk to a professional counselor. A job crisis has a way of bringing up all kinds of emotional "unfinished business" from the past. Rather than let it debilitate you, now may be the time to deal with it. Those who have done just this have been freed to pursue their dreams in a way they never could have before they passed through the fiery trial of their job crisis.

Externalize the causes of your current crisis. Don't blame yourself ("I'm no good or they would have held on to me"). Rather, try to look at the situation objectively. A recent college graduate who took many months to find a job in his field told me he became obsessed with reading the business section of the newspaper. He followed every blip in the economy because it helped him to believe that his difficulty was due not to his own weaknesses but to the recession. "It didn't make me feel too optimistic about my prospects," he admitted, "but it did help me feel better about myself."

It's easier to blame your current predicament on the economy if you were one of several people laid off because your company closed, downsized management, merged, or was acquired by another company. But it's harder to externalize the cause of your job crisis if you were fired because of something you did or if you haven't yet found your niche. Try to talk over your situation with someone who can help you see just what happened. Bob Brenner, a salesperson who was laid off despite having brought millions of dollars to the company, couldn't understand why his company terminated his job. He was told it was due to financial concerns, which he found hard to accept because he was one of the people who brought in the most money. Finally he concluded that his firing was due more to a combination of internal politics and some of his health-care expenses the company didn't want to cover. Although that was still hard to swallow, he was able to learn what he could about himself and move on without letting bitterness or shame cripple him.

Reprogram your thinking. When you notice yourself thinking those old, negative thoughts ("I'm no good. Who would want me? There must be something wrong with me. I'll never find a good job."), stop yourself. Learn to replace those old thoughts with more positive, true thoughts: "I have unique skills and abilities, and I will find a place to use them. God is in control. I am a worthy person. There is a purpose for all this."

Dr. Ronald Jensen, a therapist who counsels many people with motivation problems, says it's crucial to distinguish between thoughts and feelings. Truth is found in thoughts, not feelings. Negative messages from the past may make you feel unworthy and may even undermine the positive things you're trying to do for yourself. The key is to be aware of past messages that do not apply to the present. Now you are an adult, capable of giving yourself new messages that are truer to your reality. You are capable. You are worthy. You are lovable. You may *feel* the opposite, but remember that right feeling will eventually follow right thinking.

Reaffirm your worth. Remember that your worth and value do not depend on a job; your value comes from God. Memorize Scripture verses that affirm your intrinsic worth. One man gleaned great encouragement from Psalm 139. Another memorized this personalized paraphrase of Romans 8:38–39: "For I am convinced that neither death nor life, neither angels nor demons, neither the present nor the future, nor any powers, neither height nor depth, nor unemployment nor poverty, nor anything else in all creation, will be able to separate me from the love of God that is in Christ Jesus our Lord." Remind yourself of specific situations in which God has used you for some good. Share with a friend, spouse, or counselor your feelings about your worth. Allow them to reflect to you how they see your value. Believe them when they say you have immense value even if you are in a job crisis.

Control Your Responses and Attitudes

Part of what makes a job crisis a crisis is the sense of powerlessness. You can't control the decisions corporate America makes. But you can control plenty of things that have an impact on your job search: you can control your mental outlook, whether you will look at this as an insurmountable obstacle or an opportunity in disguise. The point of the old saying about whether the glass is half-empty or half-full is that you have control over your perspective. You can choose to believe that your job crisis has a purpose, even if you can't see it.

Decide What to Tell Others

Decide how both of you will answer *The Question:* "So, what do you do for a living?" Like Barry, you may opt to say that you are an unemployed airline pilot (pastor, banker, construction worker, executive, or whatever). Perhaps a better answer is something like, "I did X and Y, and I'm now actively looking for an opportunity to do Y." Think of ways to avoid defining yourself in terms of your job or position while still communicating what you are looking for. Giving a natural and positive answer will go a long way to help you avoid the pitfalls of isolation and shame and concentrate on one of the crucial components of job hunting, namely networking.

Learn About Yourself

No matter how painful the job crisis, it could be an opportunity in disguise. Take the time to assess yourself. What did you like about your past job? What didn't you like? What past, unfulfilled dreams may be worth another look? What would it take to make those dreams a reality? What non-job activities have you especially enjoyed in the past?

Appendix A provides a helpful tool to unlock some potential doors of opportunity. At this point, affirm this crisis as an opportunity to learn more about yourself and uncover new possibilities. This positive, hopeful attitude may help sustain you during the long process of finding work.

Organize Your Job Search

Adopt the perspective that your current focus is to deal with the crisis and get satisfactorily employed. This is your new job. Chapter 10 will explore the specific components of the job-search process. At this point, it's important to remind yourself that you do have a job to do. You may not be paid for it, but it requires just as much energy and concentration as any job you may have held. In fact, for many people, finding a job is the hardest job they will ever have. It requires a certain set of skills: research, persuasion, communication, negotiation, and interviewing techniques. Acquiring these skills is no small task. Allow yourself the time and freedom to fail as you learn them.

Reaffirm a Focus Outside Your Job Search

Get involved in one other specific thing that is important and enjoyable to you, perhaps a church commitment, a hobby, or a support group. Not only will this help to keep your job search in perspective and keep you mentally healthier, but it may lead to some job possibilities or new directions. Richard Bolles, author of *What Color Is Your Parachute?*, suggests you spend four days a week looking for a job and one day a week in some volunteer activity that helps someone who needs what you have to offer.

Continue Constructive Routines

Try to keep up a regular schedule and good health habits. Michael Catlin, during his extended job search of eighteen months, said that at some points the only thing that gave him self-respect was the fact that he got up, got dressed, and shaved every morning: "I kept up the outward appearance as far as showering and shaving and going on interviews."

Several studies on depression have shown that moderate exercise—twenty minutes a day, three or four times a week—can stave off depression. Learn techniques to keep stress manageable. Remember that you are more vulnerable to stress-related health problems: heart and gastrointestinal disorders; alcohol and drug abuse; overeating; sleep disturbance. Do whatever you can to manage your emotions and find constructive ways to cope with the stress.

Seek Professional Help If Necessary

Psychologists stress the importance of getting professional help if you find yourself sinking into continuing depression or if you find yourself unable to find pleasure in anything or if you are immobilized by anxiety. You may argue that you don't have the money for professional help. The experts say, "Find the money. You can't afford to lose perspective and emotional health." I agree. I've heard about and seen too many situations in which a husband or couple did not seek help when they clearly should have. The resulting wreckage of wasted lives and ruined relationships has no price tag. If you need help, find out if your church can help you pay at least part of the bill for a while. Find professionals who are willing to work on a sliding-scale basis. If possible, find a pastoral counselor or a church counselor who would agree to counsel you without a fee until you are through the crisis.

If you are depressed, you may not have the energy yourself to pursue these possibilities. But you can tell someone you need help and enlist their efforts to find help you can afford. This is an important time to respect your spouse's point of view. If your spouse feels that you need professional help, take her advice seriously. She may see things you are unable to see. Trust her judgment.

Bob Marone sank lower and lower into a depression because he hated his job but was not having much luck in finding something rewarding. His wife, Kerry, grew alarmed. She clearly saw the downward spiral into which he was heading: the worse he felt about himself, the less energy and confidence he possessed to find another job. The more his job prospects dwindled, the lower he sank. He needed help.

However, the Marones didn't have money to pay a professional. They were barely keeping out of debt as it was. Kerry prayed and looked for options. One day she noticed a newspaper article announcing that the university near their town was seeking volunteers for a study on depression. She and Bob applied, and Bob got free professional help.

Another couple asked for help from their church, which had a deacon's fund to cover such needs. The church set up an accountability system: the church leadership checked with the couple after an agreed-on length of time, and after deciding that the counseling was clearly helping the couple, the church extended the benefits.

Job stress has a ripple effect, spreading from the deepest place within you to the outermost edges of your life and relationships. Your wife feels that stress keenly, and one of the major challenges of surviving this time is understanding the emotional turmoil she faces as the result of your job crisis.

• 3 •

Wives Struggle Too

Ηow is Gene doing? Has he found a job yet?" a friend wanted to know after church one Sunday. Her concern was genuine; she knew that Gene had been looking for the right job for months.

I paused, speechless because of what was going on inside me. Finally I said, "He's hanging in there, but nothing's really turned up yet." What I wanted to do was scream, "He's not doing so great, and neither am I. Why doesn't anyone ever ask how I'm doing? In many ways this is just as hard on me as it is on him!"

But I didn't say it. Instead I went home and tried to bolster my husband, while secretly I wondered just how long my strength would last. I was trying to be strong enough for the two of us. But some days I wondered when the façade would crumble and I would be left gasping in the ruins.

When Vic Glavach's job search dragged on for months, his wife, Betsey, felt as if her worst nightmare had come true. "I remember the day I was lying down trying to rest when I had this vivid mental image of my head rolling off. It didn't take much to interpret that imagery: I felt as if I were coming apart. And it scared me."[1]

WIVES FEEL LOSS
AND EMOTIONAL TURMOIL

When a husband loses a job, the problem is not his alone. His wife is plunged headlong into her own crisis, one she never asked for or anticipated, and one that she is even more powerless than he is to remedy. In a way, having a spouse lose a job is similar to having one of his parents die. The loss is primarily and most immediately his, but it's also hers. His emotional reaction to the loss obviously affects her, and she too has lost something. So, just as her husband has to grieve over what he lost, she must also grieve her losses. And her losses will be different from his losses. Her losses might include her home, friends, a sense of security, a certain lifestyle, or confidence in her husband.

Chapter 2 looked inside the husband in job crisis and caught a glimpse of his pain and his feelings. While the husband is struggling with shock, relief, denial, anger, guilt, inferiority, depression, and anxiety, his wife is trying to help him. Yet she has a whole set of her own emotions to deal with, emotions she fears would only discourage her husband if she voiced them to him. So she often keeps them to herself.

What a Wife May Feel

Depending on your own personality and background, you may feel any or all of the following as you work through this process of letting go of what was and embracing what will be.

Anger. It's only natural for you to feel anger—after all, you didn't expect or invite this situation that has thrown your life into turmoil. But like your husband, you are hard pressed to know just how to direct your anger. Some wives get angry at their husbands' former boss; some lash out at their husbands. And some women, those who don't feel comfortable with anger, may bury it, only to have it come out in psychosomatic symptoms such as headaches, chronic fatigue, back pain, and ulcers. During one stressful period, when I was still in denial about how bad things really were, I experienced a chronic pain in my right lower abdomen. The doctor finally diagnosed it as spastic colon. I got medication to relieve the symptom, but knowing that stress is one common cause of spastic colon made me realize I was under more stress than I'd allowed myself to feel. Once I began to ask myself what was going on emotionally, I realized that I was holding on to a lot of anger.

Fear and anxiety. Yes, you fear all the things your husband does, and then some: What if he never gets another good job? What if you have to sell the house and move? What if you have to declare bankruptcy? What if you go back to work and the kids are ruined? What if you lose your job? What if you can't find a job either? What if one of you gets sick while you don't have health insurance? What if your car breaks down and you don't have the money to fix it? And on and on. What may make it worse for you is this: you have less control over the outcome than your husband does. You can't force him to work harder or be smarter at getting a good job; it's up to him.

Responsibility to carry the load. You may feel you have to be strong enough for the two of you. I felt this way. I didn't dare let myself feel weak or dwell on my fears lest they undermine me and then Gene too. But always having to be the strong one is a lonely role to take on. Besides, it's not even possible. I'm afraid that often my inability to allow myself to lean on Gene kept him from gathering the inner strength he did have to pull me up when I needed it.

Loss of security. The sense of having to be strong enough for both may really be a way of responding to a deeper feeling—that of losing security. "Sometimes women trap themselves in the old macho pattern even more than the men do," therapist Ruth Rosenbaum has found. "Because of the way we were all raised, it's very easy, even for an independent, financially self-sufficient woman, to feel a loss of security and a loss of love."[2]

If your husband was the sole financial support of the family, you are bound to feel your security threatened. But even if both of you work, your husband's lack of a steady job will shake your sense that you can depend on your husband financially.

Loss of respect. For Lisa Ellis, a thirty-eight-year-old newspaper reporter, an unemployed husband recalled the image of her unemployed father. When Lisa's husband, Bill, would lie around in bed in the morning, all she could see was the specter of her father, clad in pajamas, rocking in the rocking chair, and listening to a ball game on the radio. Though Bill always got up and got dressed in the morning, to Lisa he still symbolized a frighteningly weak man.

Besides that, she didn't agree with his attitude. He believed that his position as a photographer was eliminated not because he wasn't talented but because he was too original, too independent, and his boss had felt threatened. This attitude infuriated Lisa. Bill was evoking what cultural anthropologist Katherine Newman calls the "manly flaw" theory of unemployment: he lost his job because he was unwilling to bend and play political games.

Several couples described similar dynamics. To the wives, such an attitude seems like so much male hype. But Newman warns against dismissing a partner's manly-flaw defenses. First, people erect defenses in a crisis because they need them. Second, they may be right to some degree. Newman cites a 1980 British managerial unemployment study that compared the personality characteristics of unemployed executives with those of a control group of employed executives. The study showed that the unemployed executives were indeed more assertive, conscientious, imaginative, independent, and self-sufficient than those who were employed.[3]

Lisa needed to separate her current situation from her own insecurities stemming from the past. Bill was doing part-time, free-lance work and saying he preferred working for himself. Though this made Lisa uncomfortable, she needed to see that Bill was really very unlike her father.

Disappointment and the loss of dreams. Sometimes we don't even realize we have a dream until it appears it will never happen. I didn't know how strongly I craved security, for instance, until I had to face the possibility that Gene and I never would be financially secure. I also had the dream of having several children. For a long time I didn't see how we could afford even one. It appeared I would always have to work full time, if not be the sole wage-earner. I didn't feel I wanted to have a child I saw only at night, when I was exhausted, or on weekends. Grappling to accept what seemed a chronic problem—underemployment—meant letting go of some dreams.

Other women have had to let go of the dream of a comfortable retirement or of the dream of mothering their children full time when the children are young. Some women have to give up their dreams by giving up a job they love in order to relocate.

Envy. Some wives feel envious when they are working to support their family, and their husbands have all kinds of free time. Martha Catlin said, "I had all these projects I wanted to get done; I wished I could have had all the time Michael had."

I vividly remember the day I called Gene from work in the middle of the day. After several rings, he answered the phone sleepily. He was napping, in the middle of the day! Here I was, slaving away at my job; wouldn't I have loved to take a nap too. I felt furious, a fury born of envy.

You also may struggle with envy for other women who do not have financial worries. "It's very difficult for me to visit some of my friends," one woman confessed to me. "I have a hard time not comparing. And I come home feeling more discontented over the way we have to live."

Lack of sexual desire. Though some wives are able to separate the job crisis from their sexual feelings, many find that anger, resentment, or their own feelings about their husbands' unemployment all conspire to undermine their sexual feelings. In addition, if their husbands are having problems sexually, they may misunderstand and feel rejected. This can start a negative cycle in an area that has the potential for bringing joy and healing.

Resentment. Again, because you didn't cause this discomfort and cannot alleviate it, you may resent the changes you're forced to make. Carl Griffin left the pastorate and spent several years working odd jobs while looking for another career. Gina went back to work full time to keep them afloat financially. She resented Carl for not getting a better-paying job so she could stay home with their two preschoolers.

Other women resent having to bear the consequences of a husband's unwise decisions or changing their lifestyle or having their "territory" invaded or coping with a disrupted or altered social life.

Like anger, resentment is a potential poison. Denying it won't help; it will just erupt somehow. Acknowledging it, confessing it to God, and trying to change your perspective is the only way out.

Although these feelings may frighten you, I hope that describing them here will help you admit your own feelings and know that you are not alone. I also hope that understanding a wife's feelings described here and a husband's feelings described in chapter 2 will help both of you understand what your spouse may be going through, even though he or she may not find it easy to admit to the feelings. Having a glimpse at what your spouse may be feeling may change your own feelings toward the other and enable you to begin to work together, as a team, to get through this.

That's what happened with me. It took me a long time to confront my feelings about Gene's job struggles. The hardest hurdle was the respect issue. Steeped as I was in the work ethic, respect was bound up in achievement. Surely, if one door was closed, he could find something else.

We argued about it—often. One night things came to a head. That is when Gene cried out, "You don't know what it's like for me because you've never failed!" I felt for the first time his despair. Gene had opened the door to his heart, and I had fallen in. I found it a very lonely, frightening, discouraging place to be. I knew Gene felt small in the eyes of others for not having a thriving career. And here I was, in essence mimicking their attitude! At the same time, I still struggled with the respect issue.

Unable to sleep, I got up at five o'clock and took a walk. I prayed hard—confused prayers, anguished prayers. And slowly an answer came: I can respect him for his *struggle*.

I had been concentrating on the wrong thing—his "failure." But now that I saw how agonizing his struggle was, I found something that commanded tremendous respect: that he was hanging in there and fighting. He could choose to opt out, like many men I knew, through any number of means: alcohol, drugs, extramarital sex. But my husband was not giving up—he kept hoping, kept looking, kept working. Once I experienced, from the inside, how lonely and discouraged he felt, I realized what tremendous strength it took to keep fighting and not give up.

That moment changed our relationship.

I encourage both of you to look over the lists of feelings again and decide which are the biggest issues for you. If you're the husband, go back to chapter 2 and devise an action plan for dealing with the issues you struggle with most. If you're the wife reading this, start praying specifically about your top issues. It may seem as if the crisis is largely the husband's to solve, but wives have a tremendous influence. With the couples I interviewed, it was sometimes the wife who had some kind of breakthrough—always through prayer—that led to freedom for the husband to do what he had to do.

Not only does a job crisis place unusual stress on you and your spouse as individuals, but it also strains your marriage. To keep your marriage healthy during a job crisis, you will need to face some predictable stress points in your marriage. The next chapter will outline those stress points and explore ways you can move toward each other during the crisis rather than distance yourselves from each other and inflict deeper wounds.

· 4 ·

Marriage in Turmoil and Triumph

One of the problems about unemployment or constant underemployment is that the couple doesn't know how long it will last. Bearing up under stress is much easier when the end is in sight. The uncertainty of unemployment itself saps strength and strains the marriage. As Martha Catlin put it, the eighteen months her husband was out of work was a "drought, both in terms of his career goals and in terms of our marriage."

But Martha and her husband survived. So did Vic and Betsey Glavach, whose "drought" also lasted for a year and a half. My marriage had survived eight years of Gene battling underemployment and unemployment. What we couples have learned is that job stress can make our marriages stronger than ever.

But not before we first passed through the fire.

When we were going through that fire, we didn't know if we would survive. We didn't know if it would consume us; it had consumed some marriages.

But it need not. You can do several things to ensure that the fire of a job crisis will not burn and destroy you.

THE SEESAW EFFECT

When a husband loses a job, he feels the effects immediately. The wife may be in shock too, but for a while she focuses on helping him deal with his intense emotions and bolstering his confidence. Studies show that wives' psychological and health problems tend to peak around six months after their husbands' problems do.[1]

This means that a husband and wife may not be dealing with the same kinds of issues at the same time. For instance, a husband may be coping with deep feelings of shame and grieving his losses while a wife is working on the practical issues of how they're going to cut back, whether or not she should go back to work if she's not already employed, or how they will rearrange household labor now that her husband is home most of the time. Then, after the husband has sorted through his emotions somewhat, the wife may begin to feel the loss of social contacts, frustrations about how her husband is conducting his job search, or fear for their future.

Betsey Glavach described the tensions she and Vic had to work out because of their different needs. "I'd come home from work (I eventually took a full-time job), and I'd want to talk about what contacts Vic had made that day, the leads that looked good. I wanted to hear any sign of encouragement and hope. But by the end of the day Vic was ready to quit thinking about the job search. He felt badgered by my questions and more of a failure for not having found a job yet."[2]

It's not always a bad thing for a couple to be in a different place emotionally, however. The emotional seesaw also worked positively for Vic and Betsey. Vic described a typical week, which also characterized many of the couples I talked to. "When I was down, Betsey helped pull me up, and when she was down, I'd do the same for her. She'd be fine all week while I was getting more and more discouraged with all the negative results of my search. Her encouragement would keep me going. When the weekends came, I'd be able to set my discouragement aside, knowing I'd done my best all week and needed to relax and let go of the stress if I was going to have the strength I needed again the next week. So I'd feel positive enough to encourage her when she hit bottom on the weekends."[3]

Another variation of the seesaw effect occurs when one spouse evades an issue and the other wants to confront it head on. Patty Selneck felt this frustration with her husband, who had a history of unfulfilling jobs although he had a master's degree. Her husband, Jeff, would feel the need to get a job, any job, just to alleviate the pain of unemployment. She, however, saw a pattern repeat itself and felt he should take some time to assess what he really wanted to do with his life.

In cases like this, it doesn't matter who is right and who is wrong. If you find yourself in a deadlock over some issue, try to step back and look objectively at what is happening. Often the problem is that you are each at different places, wrestling with different issues. Once you recognize that, you can either try to talk out what is happening or wait until you come to a point of greater equilibrium before you try to work it out.

AS THE SEARCH DRAGS ON

If a job crisis does not end after the first several months, new issues will begin to creep into your relationship. You will have to come to grips with your financial situation, which is never easy. This may mean going out less often with other couples, so your social life will decrease at just the time you most need other people's support. Or, if you were used to socializing with people from the workplace, those relationships are often too uncomfortable to maintain after a job loss.

Both of you may find that old problems and resentments

that were easy to bury beneath a hectic lifestyle may suddenly demand attention. Perhaps you never helped around the house before, but now that both of you are home all the time, your spouse can't bear it anymore. Or perhaps one of you is a spendthrift, which wasn't much of a problem until now, when you have to watch your money so carefully. Maybe your spouse isn't neat, but you were able to overlook it before. Now that both of you share the same work space, the messy house continually gets on your nerves.

Ken Potts, a psychologist practicing in the Chicago area, points out that some couples try to solve their problems through creating distance between them. For instance, if a couple had sexual problems before the job crisis, the problems may have easily been masked by a busy lifestyle that left both spouses too busy and tired to have sex very often. But now that they have more time and opportunity for intimacy, the problem may no longer be avoidable. Or perhaps spouses never really agreed on how to discipline the children, but they worked it out by never disciplining them at the same time; the parent at hand would take care of the problem in his or her own way. Now, however, if Dad is home much of the time, the husband and wife need to work out their differences.

Role Changes

Most couples I interviewed indicated they had problems because both spouses were home during the day. The husbands often didn't know what to do with themselves. And the wives resented their husbands' "invasion" of their turf. Mona Parrish, who had three young children and did not work outside the home, found it difficult to have her husband around all the time. It was a sudden, unwelcome disruption of her routine. "I lost my territory, my space," she said. "Friends didn't feel as free to come over."

Even wives who worked outside the home and whose

husbands had always helped with household chores felt the strain of having their husbands home all the time. Les and Alice Falen discovered this, much to their surprise. Even though Les had often cooked before he was unemployed, that activity took on a different significance in Alice's mind once Les was unemployed. They recalled the "pie incident."

Les decided to treat everybody and make a pie. It would be a gift, something he could do for the family as a treat, now that he had time on his hands. He looked up the recipe and made an apple pie.

Alice, however, was not pleased when she got home from her job and saw Les' handiwork. In fact, she was furious! Les felt bewildered that she could get so worked up over a simple little thing like Les' pie. Alice admitted that if he had done this when he had been employed, she would have thought it was wonderful. But in the context of his unemployment, Alice felt it was one more instance of Lee taking over more and more of her "stuff." She said, "I want to be home making pies. You should be out working. I want you out of my space!"

The Falens had to work through their differing needs for distance and closeness through honestly communicating their needs. At first Alice just kept backing off, and Les felt bewildered and rejected. After they talked through what was happening, they understood their reactions better.

Tensions over role changes may surprise a couple. I thought Gene and I were very "liberated," and we were, compared to many couples. Who did what around the house was never an issue; we worked out an equitable arrangement comfortable to both of us. I always enjoyed my work and couldn't imagine it not being a part of my life. But during Gene's periods of unemployment, when I was the main wage-earner, I didn't like that role. The context was different; suddenly I had no choice about whether or not I worked. I guess I was like the 500 American women who took part in a study in the late 1980s on how American and Swedish wives viewed the role of wage-earner. American women preferred to view that role as an option, not as an obligation, and they expressed discontent when they felt forced to be the main wage-earners. Swedish women, on the other hand, saw themselves as being obligated to contribute to their families' income.[4]

Whose Job Comes First?

Tensions may arise when the wife becomes the wage-earner, but they may also arise when the husband and wife disagree about other financial issues. If the husband thinks the wife should get a job and she doesn't want to, they will experience tension in their relationship. When the wife already works, the issue of whose career is primary comes into play if the husband considers a job move.

George and Geri Talman have been married for four years. Geri is a vice-president in a publishing company; George just finished college. When his job search dragged on for several months, with prospects in his field looking bleaker and bleaker, the issue of relocation came up. And with it came some conflict, especially for Geri. "My experience is in the corporate setting," she said. "What if we moved to a small town and I couldn't find a job?"

The real issue for the Talmans, and for other couples in this dilemma, is whose career comes first. George reasoned that since Geri had already experienced career success, it was his turn. Since Geri had enjoyed career success in a couple of different fields, he was confident she would find another good job if they had to move. Besides, hadn't they agreed that someday they wanted to have children and that she would stay home with them while they were young? Well then, it's clear that his career would come first at this point.

Geri agreed with all this in her head, but the possibility

of giving up a job she loved and moving still made her choke. But when she finally accepted it and was able to tell George she was willing to move if that's what it took, George did not take it lightly.

While possible relocation is a dilemma for some couples, almost all couples feel another recurring tension: the husband and wife will almost inevitably have different views on how the husband should conduct his job search.

Whose Job Hunt Is It, Anyway?

"Everyone has a model of what they would do if they were unemployed: the eagerness, the thoroughness, the energy with which they would do it," observes Judith Sills, a Philadelphia-based therapist. "It's almost inevitable your partner won't do it the way you would. And to the extent that he doesn't conform to your model, you'll feel angry."[5]

I have read articles that advised women to take a very active role in their husband's job search. I don't think that's a good idea for most couples. I have found that if the wife steps in and tries to control too much, it will only delay her husband's process of finding another job. A wife's active involvement may threaten the husband's confidence and judgment. What may be a wife's good advice may not be the right advice for her husband.

Geri Talman learned this after a painful confrontation. Trying to be helpful, she would go through the classified section of the Sunday newspaper and circle anything that looked promising for George. But when he would follow up only five of her twenty leads, she felt frustrated. Why was he narrowing the field? she fumed. He would answer that he didn't feel qualified for some of those jobs. She patiently explained that ads describe the ideal candidates, and often an employer has to settle for less. She should know—she has placed ads and hired people herself, many times. After a while

George began to second-guess himself—an occupational hazard of the job search. "Maybe if I had followed up on some of those leads Geri had circled, I'd have a job by now," he would think. That sapped his confidence in himself. Finally, he asked Geri just to lay off, to leave the job search entirely to him. And that proved the wisest course.

If you're the wife, you may feel your husband should be accountable to you for how his job search is progressing, especially if he is not accountable to anyone else. You wonder, *Should I nag or keep quiet? Where is the line between nagging and giving a needed kick in the pants?* But psychologist Ken Potts believes it's best to keep out of it altogether, and I agree. When I interfered too much in Gene's employment struggles, making them my own as well as his, I inadvertently set up all kinds of dynamics that just sapped the energy Gene needed to look for better work.

Chapter 11 will list some concrete suggestions for how wives *can* help their husbands in their job search. For now, wives, trust me: stay out of the job-search process. Give advice only if your husband asks it. Let this be *his* job search, his problem. Trust him to solve it on his own.

Another related tension arises if the husband and wife hold different ideas of achievement and how to go about attaining it. As Margie, a successful executive at age thirty-two, told me, "You decide what you want, you go after it, and you get it."

But here's the rub: Margie's husband, Bill, has been unable to achieve his dream. For the past ten years he has tried to break into his field. He has experienced periods of unemployment. Now he holds a job he hates while he continues to look for more satisfying work. Margie can't understand why "The System" worked for her and not for her husband.

When Rob Geisler decided to volunteer to be laid off and take a sabbatical to catch up on some of the rest of his life, his wife, Joan, had a hard time understanding it. She came from an achievement-oriented family, and jumping ship without another place to land just didn't make sense to her. But she accepted his plan not to look for another job through the fall months. Yet as the months dragged on and he still wasn't looking actively for a job, Joan got worried. In her mind, the sabbatical was time-linked: he would find a job at the end of fall.

In Rob's mind, his sabbatical was linked to certain tasks he wanted to finish. Because a generous severance package meant Rob had no financial pressure to get a job right away, life had a way of filling up his time. Getting more involved with his son, taking on extra responsibilities at church left him seemingly little time to look for a job. And will he be less employable the longer he took to jump back into the fray? Those were big questions in Joan's mind and an underlying source of tension in their marriage.

Money Pressures and . . .

Rob and Joan were unusual. For most couples facing an employment crisis, finances loom as one of the main concerns and continuing sources of tension. Money problems can set off the panic button for husband or wife. Tight finances may mean giving up a cherished home, the community where you have laid down deep roots, a certain lifestyle. Any of these losses may lead to resentment, especially resentment by the wife toward her husband.

But money is also inevitably symbolic. To some people, it symbolizes security and freedom. To others it's a sign of status. Whatever money has come to mean to you on an emotional level, you will have to mourn that loss in some way. Sometimes the crisis forces you to face for the first time what money really means to you.

To Derek Halstad, money meant social status. He earned

a good salary as manager of a shoe store. He bought a big house, two cars, and a grand piano. But Derek also wanted more satisfaction than he found in his present job, and he changed careers to work for a fledgling company that tried to help Third-World countries. But when that company collapsed, Derek was out of work. His wife, Karen, took care of their three children and did some waitressing on the side, but they lost their house, their cars, nearly everything they owned.

It devastated Derek. He felt ruined not only financially but also socially. He so dreaded *The Question*—"What do you do for a living?"—that he constructed an elaborate system of denial. "Derek would tell people we were doing great. He would prep me on what to say to people," Karen said. The façade and the social isolation wore Karen down.

Social Isolation

This may be one of the worst aspects of unemployment: the social isolation that can result, either because the husband and wife deliberately try to hide the truth, as the Halstads did, or because they slip out of their social loop simply because they no longer have the money to do what they used to do with friends. Mona Parrish said that she doesn't ask people over for dinner anymore because the family's food budget is so tight. And now the invitations to her family have also slowed down.

If the husband and wife don't agree on how open to be, they will find the tension between them increasing. It's not always the husband who hides out, either. Bob Brenner openly told anyone and everyone he was looking for a job, figuring that the more people knew, the quicker he would find a lead to a job. His wife, Gail, theoretically agreed with Bob, but emotionally she didn't feel comfortable with his openness.

You must intensely fight to avoid social isolation because support from others is critical at this time. At times during an employment crisis, a husband and wife will have nothing left to give each other. All their energy is consumed with coping.

WAYS COUPLES TRY TO COPE

Some of the following coping mechanisms may work, some won't. I'm including those I encountered, both good and bad, so that wherever you are in your journey, you can know that others have stood in your shoes. Even though you feel alone, even though you feel you should be handling this better, take comfort in knowing that other people have faced the same crisis. Just as other people have gone through the valley and have come out again, so can you—no matter how far down you feel you are at the moment.

Fighting

Fighting, of course, is a common way of releasing tension. Several couples said that they fought a lot more during the job crisis, often over little things. The couples who continually committed themselves to the marriage made sure they resolved the fight before it lasted too long, however. The couples whose marriage plunged into trouble were never able to get at the real issues or resolve their conflicts. They did not "fight fair." Instead, they blamed and attacked the other until trust crumbled.

Gail Brenner remembered lashing out at Bob when he failed to stop at a red light in time. She let loose all the fear and anger she felt over losing her sense of security. To Gail at the moment, Bob's action seemed like just one more instance of his irresponsibility. To her it felt as if he were putting the family's security in danger. Bob sat there, stunned but unable to defend himself. He knew he had let her and the family down, and he already felt sorry about it.

Expect to fight more during a job crisis, but work hard at

trying to get at the real issues. And be careful how you fight. Ken Potts suggests that couples express feeling statements before they state information or ask questions: "I feel angry and worried when I see you just sitting in front of the television hour after hour. What's going on?" This kind of confrontation can enhance communication. It's difficult, because it requires you to first get in touch with some scary feelings that are easier to deny than to face. But calling your husband a lazy bum for watching television all the time, or your wife a nag, does nothing but tear the other down and build higher walls between you.

Try hard not to let the arguments deteriorate into blaming each other. You may be able to find plenty of reasons for blame. Some women blame their husbands for losing the job or for not looking hard enough for another one. Some husbands blame their wives for not being willing to go back to work. (Though most of the time, the wife lashes out at the husband and the husband accepts the blame because he already feels bad about himself.)

Trying to Control Each Other

The husband may try to control how much others know about their situation, as was true with the Halstads. Or the wife may try to control her husband's job search. The more threatened and out of control a person feels, the more he or she may try to control the situation. And if the husband appears passive because he's depressed, the wife may feel so terrified that she steps in and tries to take over in the guise of "helping."

For a while Kerry Marone tried very hard to "make Bob happy." He was so unhappy in his job that she tried to do anything and everything to make him happy at home. But Kerry's desire to please Bob turned into an unhealthy pattern of control. It wasn't until Kerry learned to step back and let

Bob take responsibility for his own feelings that their marriage turned back toward health.

Trying to Escape

Thoughts of escape are natural, and our culture certainly encourages escape rather than perseverance. Several people I knew hinted that maybe I should consider divorcing Gene. Betsey Glavach remembered how the pain seemed endless the second summer of Vic's unemployment. When she tried to imagine what she could do to escape the pain, the only escape she could see was to divorce Vic and get away from it all. Though she determined not to let the experience destroy her marriage, the thought was still there.

Our culture offers a plethora of other opportunities to escape our problems: drugs, alcohol, entertainment, food. One man recalled watching videos almost constantly when he was unemployed. Other people may fall prey to spending sprees, especially if they receive a good severance package, as a way of denying and escaping the reality of their plight.

While healthy forms of escape are important stress reducers, beware of anything that becomes habitual. If either of you had a problem before in any of these areas, the temptation will be even stronger now. Take precautions and be alert to signs that you or your spouse may need further help.

Talking It Out

Couples who are used to sharing their feelings and accepting their spouse's feelings may find that a job crisis brings them closer together. Roberta Schaefer would come home from the grocery store and throw herself in her husband's arms and sob over the frustration of not having enough money to feed their family of seven. Kyle accepted her feelings—she wasn't blaming him, just continuing their previous pattern of talking out their feelings. He let her know that he loved her no matter what. That kind of unconditional love, she says, has gone a long way toward keeping them together in this crisis and even healing some old wounds from her past.

Pulling Back

As psychologist Ken Potts pointed out, one common way to deal with stress is to pull back emotionally. Both of you—or only one of you—may feel that coping with your own feelings consumes all the energy you have. Bob Marone remembered days and days when he returned home from a job he hated feeling so drained that he simply didn't have the energy to conduct a job search. Other men who hated their jobs reported similar feelings: they simply had little energy left for their families. Conversely, if the wife is trying to come to grips with her feelings about her husband's situation, she may not feel able to be open with him.

Allowing each other some space can be very healthy. Mitch Grisweiler was grateful that Pam didn't always press him to share his feelings because for one thing, he wasn't always sure he knew what he was feeling. For another, he didn't always have the energy to bring her into his struggles.

And if the truth is told, we don't always have the energy or desire to receive our spouse's emotions either. "The first time Vic became depressed, it terrified me," Betsey Glavach admitted. "What if he doesn't come out of this? What can I do to bring him out of it? The fear was horrendous."[6]

I remember going through the same thing with Gene. After a while, I think we learned to hide our emotions in an attempt to protect each other. I wasn't sure I could handle Gene's deepest, darkest emotions. I also wasn't sure I wanted to face my own enough to admit them to Gene.

Protecting each other from our feelings is not all bad. The real test is whether you stop communicating at all. Martha Catlin felt that Michael built a wall between them that she couldn't break down. She said, "We weren't communicating. We loved each other, but I couldn't touch him. I couldn't reach out and break through the wall that he had built up to protect me from his depression. He had no other outlet for that."

Understanding your emotions and your stress points as a couple enables you to develop the coping strategies that have allowed certain couples to survive and even thrive. Here are the survival tactics those of us in the trenches have hammered out.

MARRIAGE SURVIVAL TACTICS

The couples whose marriages grew during their struggles with a job crisis worked on two key areas: they found a way to maintain or restore respect, and they overcame denial and isolation. In addition to these areas, other couples found help in re-negotiating the underlying contract, serving each other, verbalizing empathy, allowing each other the freedom to fail, practicing forgiveness, facing financial realities together, strengthening their faith, and renewing their commitment to each other.

Redefine Respect

The husbands and wives who remained tied to one-dimensional definitions of success and failure often lost respect for themselves or their spouses. If you have lost respect for yourself or your spouse, do whatever you can to redefine respect. Adjust your values. Find new and true things for which to respect your spouse.

In this process, a wife's influence is immense. If she

focuses on her husband's positive qualities and repeatedly affirms them to him, he begins to see beyond the world's definition of success and failure. "I grew in respect for my husband," Pam Grisweiler said. "I saw how hard Mitch worked at getting a job. I saw how he used his time to serve others in their need. I saw how he continued to give back to God, through tithing what little we had."

Martha Catlin moved from pity to respect for her husband, Michael, as she focused less on his outward identity and more on his inner qualities. "Michael is a son of God. Michael is my husband. Michael is a fellow human being who is going through some rough times and needs a friend." She also consciously looked for her husband's strong points and found many. "Michael has an amazing ability to manage finances. During the three periods of his unemployment, we weren't strapped financially, mostly because of his ability to squeeze a penny and make it scream three times before he let go."

Redefining the basis for respect is an ongoing process for both spouses. It may take years for the husband to get over the emotional trauma of not having a career—even once he finds his niche and succeeds in it. Michael Catlin and Derek Halstad both have good jobs now, jobs they've succeeded in for three or more years. Yet their past "failures" still haunt them, and they speak of their pain in the present tense. Still, though the scars remain, they have broadened their definitions of themselves. Michael is more, now, than a banker: he is also a follower of Christ, a husband, father, friend to other men who struggle.

Overcome Denial and Isolation

Spouses who continue to deny the reality of their struggle cut off communication not only with outsiders but also with each other. Denial and isolation eat away at the individual and the marriage.

Share your fears and doubts with someone other than your spouse. Your spouse can't carry your load and his or hers as well. Don't hide out. Find at least one other confidant with whom you can be honest.

Give each other room to work through painful feelings. Because distancing is one way to deal with a crisis, it should not have surprised me to find that many of the couples didn't talk directly about their difficulties while they were going through the crisis. Mitch Grisweiler said, "I was glad Pam didn't probe too deeply into what I was feeling. I wasn't sure I could handle talking about it with her." But he had a rock-solid trust that his wife believed in him and sympathized with his struggle. And they did continue to communicate in other areas.

This is the key to knowing whether or not the distancing is healthy. Ask yourself: Do we communicate our feelings about other things, even if right now we can't always tell each other our deepest feelings? If the answer is no, then you need to work on whatever problems may be blocking you from working through this together.

Don't be afraid to seek help. Many couples I interviewed sought professional help. Some opted for individual therapy, others for marriage counseling, and still others for career counseling for the husband. Sometimes, if supportive friends and family are not available, professional help is the only recourse.

How do you know if you need help? If you can't communicate about anything, if you or your spouse is building thicker and thicker walls, if one or both are immobilized by anxiety or depression—then you need help. If a person is so depressed that he or she can't find pleasure in anything, that's a warning sign. If there is talk of "ending it all," get immediate help!

Other Survival Tactics

Re-negotiate the underlying contract. Several psychologists point out that all relationships operate by certain unwritten, unspoken contracts. When a radical change like a job crisis occurs, all those contracts are up for grabs. Contracts about parenting, household responsibilities, money, and the spouse's involvement in the job search—all need to be re-negotiated. Psychotherapist Ken Potts suggests that couples get as concrete as possible when talking out these practical issues. Don't say, "I'll help more around the house." Rather, say something like, "Since I don't have a job right now, I want to budget twenty-five hours a week for my job search, five more for travel. That leaves me ten extra hours to do some jobs around the house. How about if I cook two meals a week and take over the grocery shopping, laundry, and vacuuming?" In re-negotiating contracts, Potts suggests you be as specific and measurable as possible. Hammering out contracts about the practical issues that bother you will help lessen any resentment or feeling of unfairness.

Serve each other. Remember the seesaw effect: when one spouse feels low, the other is usually up. If both of you feel down, make an extra effort to put the other's needs before your own. "We learned that love is a choice, an act of the will," Martha and Michael Catlin said.

Verbalize empathy. One day Geri Talman came home from work and saw a stack of note cards with names, phone numbers, and notes on each. It was George's list of contacts he'd made, or attempted to make, during that day. Looking at his notes, she put herself in his shoes and realized how difficult it must be to pick up the phone every day and call strangers to try to find job leads.

But she didn't stop there: she told George what she felt. "It meant a lot to me to hear her say she realized how hard it was to find a job," George said.

Do whatever you can to sensitize yourself to what your spouse is going through, and verbalize your empathy. That is one way to allow your spouse to open up if he or she needs to share feelings.

Give each other the freedom to fail, to be weak. This more than anything else can communicate the kind of unconditional love your spouse craves at this time. I marvel that Kyle Schaefer did not get defensive when Roberta came home and sobbed in his arms about how hard it is to grocery shop with too little money. But Kyle's unconditional love freed Roberta to love him back, and it tempered their marriage.

Vic Glavach told Betsey that he needed to be able to talk to her, even when his feelings might be distressing. Eventually they got to the point where he was able to "cry like a baby" one night while they were lying in bed, and Betsey remained calm. She just held and encouraged Vic. That proved to him that he could depend on her—even when he felt he was losing control.

Practice forgiveness. When employment stress plagues a marriage for months or years on end, both partners will make poor decisions at times. Sometimes the husband may make a bad decision that sets him back. Or the wife may say too much to a friend, leaving a husband feeling betrayed. Sometimes practicing forgiveness was a daily exercise for Gene and me. Yet each time we forgave the other, something subtle but substantial happened: whatever wall we happened to be constructing came tumbling down.

Face the financial facts together. Sometimes finances will be worse than you thought, but sometimes you may find you have assets you had overlooked. "What the couple needs to do is to get away from the symbolism [of money] and confront the financial reality," therapist Ruth Rosenbaum advises.[7] One woman found that she and her husband had a comfortable cushion of savings in the bank and a mortgage that was manageable on her salary alone. The husband's wealthy parents had already set up a trust fund to pay for their grandchildren's education—if and when the couple had a child. The wife wanted to start a family, but when her husband was laid off, she felt afraid to become pregnant. Facing the financial facts convinced her that her security was not as threatened as she originally imagined.

Sit down as soon as possible and make out a bare-bones budget that will allow you to live on the wife's salary and/or unemployment compensation for as long as possible before tapping into savings or any severance package the husband may receive. Too many horror stories tell of professional people remaining unemployed for months on end, when the couple was certain a good job was just around the corner. Be conservative and spend your money after you find a job.

Keep at least one area of your life unspoiled by the stress. Find something you can continue to enjoy together without the overtones of your crisis coloring it. Gene and I delighted together over our young son, having fun as a family. Gene is a wonderful father, and I was always able to affirm that. I sometimes had to work at not letting some of our struggles color this area of our lives, but it became quite a refuge and place of bonding.

The Glavaches said they came to a deeper appreciation for sex; they saw it as a real gift they could give each other. It served as an escape and helped hold them together, Betsey said. "It reminded us that something in life was still wonderful by allowing us times to forget the troubles and just experience joy."[8]

Do whatever you can to strengthen your faith. When anxiety attacks—and it does, often, for couples who don't have steady employment—sometimes it feels as if all you have to hang on to are God's promises. Martha Catlin said, "I kept remembering over and over that God is in control, and that he knew our needs, he knew Michael's needs, not just financial but emotional, psychological, and spiritual." Several husbands and wives regularly reminded each other of all the provisions they did see: old cars and appliances that didn't break down, good health, odd jobs coming their way, friends who invited them over for dinner, loans from family members.

Renew your commitment often. At odd moments the vows I made at our wedding ceremony popped into my head: "For better or worse, for richer or poorer. . . ." I'd laugh bitterly to myself, thinking, "Well, this is certainly for worse and for poorer." But the implicit challenge of the vow never failed to stimulate new resolve, maybe because I'm just not a quitter. Other couples said their commitment to each other laid a foundation of security on which they could build a shelter for themselves and each other. Bob Marone said, "Kerry and I have grown closer as a couple because we went through this hardship. If another one comes along, I know that we can make it. It's like a pat on the back as a couple because you've survived the crisis."

Practicing these steps will also go a long way to enabling you to help your children weather this drought. Getting your relationship on a firm footing can set the stage for a time when the whole family can pull together and share some very special times.

· 5 ·

Families Pulling Together

Rick Wilson, twelve years old, lives in an affluent suburb outside a midwestern city. When his dad first lost his job as part of work-force reduction at his company six months earlier, Rick said he was afraid "that we wouldn't have enough to eat and we wouldn't have nice things."

Thirteen-year-old Anita Moore said she waited more than three months before telling her best friend that her father had been laid off from his job as a transportation manager. "I found myself not wanting to tell people about Dad being unemployed," Anita said. "When I think of unemployed people, I think of people out on the street."

If you have children, no doubt your situation is complicated by your concerns for how your employment crisis will affect them. Suddenly you—and they—are faced with problems that low-income families face—how to pay for housing, utilities, medical care, and food. The shock is there for them as well as you. Eight-year-old Lindsey, Anita's sister, remembers watching a television program in which kids talked about what it was like to have a parent not working and the financial pressures that resulted. "I used to think they were different from me," Lindsey said. "Now it's easy to understand what the kids were saying."

LIFE WILL NEVER BE QUITE THE SAME

"Unemployment will either draw a family together or pull it apart," observes Tom Morton, author of *The Survivor's Guide to Unemployment*. "Rarely do families remain the same when a breadwinner loses a job."[1]

Acknowledging that life for you and your family will not be the same is the first step toward turning a job crisis into a positive experience. One woman recalled a turnaround in her attitude—and her family's experience of her husband's unemployment—when she realized that God wanted to use this career pitfall to bring the family closer to him. "This layoff is God's plan," she affirmed to her family. "If we look for them, we'll see God's blessings."

A family can pull together, but only if it recognizes and deals positively with the stresses each family member experiences and with the impact each member has on the others. Many family counselors liken the family to a mobile, with each piece linked to the others and to the whole in such a way that one slight tremor will set the whole mobile trembling. And a job crisis is no small tremor. It's as if someone has grabbed the wage-earner and almost wrenches him from the mobile. Not only is that member bent, but the whole mobile flails around.

FAMILY DYNAMICS DURING A JOB CRISIS

What are you—parents and children—thinking, feeling, and doing during this time of job crisis? Beware of the negative dynamics that develop during a job crisis. But also be aware of some positive family dynamics that can result from your situation.

Fear of Having Children

If you do not already have children or if you dreamed of adding to your family, an employment crisis may make you wonder if you can afford a child. During the years when Gene's job situation was unstable, I was very reluctant to start a family. I didn't want to work full time if we had a child; I didn't want to be in a position where I would have no choice but to work full time yet not be able to afford quality day-care, occasional meals out, or the housecleaning help that seemed to me the only way to manage a two-paycheck lifestyle. (Superwoman I am not!) Perhaps the real issue was that at the time I instinctively felt I would not have the emotional energy parenthood would demand.

The Catlins felt the same way. "We knew we could survive with just the two of us," Martha said. "If we had to tighten the belts another notch, that would be okay. But to add that to the natural stresses of marriage and a new baby—that would be too much."

Nevertheless, the Catlins felt the old "biological clock" exerting its pressure and decided to start a family. Martha got pregnant while Michael was still out of a job. Then she miscarried. Although that was hard for them, they also believed there must be a reason it happened. Later they did come to see some sense in it because Martha was able to take a three-month work assignment out of town, an assignment she never would have done had she had a baby.

Some couples dream of having a family or enlarging their family, but they don't see how they can manage economically. Now as the job crisis drags on, they feel their dream crumbling. This is yet another loss to bear and to grieve.

Fear of How Family Might React

If you do have children, you no doubt are concerned about the effect your crisis will have on your children. And rightly so. Every family member will react. Whether they react positively or negatively is partly up to how you and your spouse respond.

You may fear that the children will feel shamed. Much of Larry Penney's anguish over his unemployment stemmed from a desire not to see his children hurt. "I don't want their classmates saying, 'Nah-nah-nah, your father's out of work,'" he said. But this fear may be more a reflection of your own attitudes than your child's. Larry's fifteen-year-old daughter shrugged off his fear: "My boyfriend's dad was a McDonald's executive, and he just lost his job," she said. To her, her father's job loss was something unpleasant, but it wasn't a cause for deep embarrassment.

You may wonder how this experience will affect your children's view of work, especially if your kids are older. Will they come to view important events in their lives as out of control? How do you pass on a good work ethic when it seems as if it didn't work for you?

You may also worry about the reaction of your extended family. One man said he couldn't get up the nerve to tell his own father about his unemployment until after he found another job. You may fear feeling pressured or misunderstood by your extended family.

Resentment and Anger

A job crisis is a breeding ground for resentment and anger. You blow up when your children cry and make demands. You resent that you can't even meet their basic needs for food, clothing, shelter, and transportation. You may resent their whining and complaining. You may even resent it if your parents or your spouse's parents try to help by offering money—or if they *don't* offer.

If you do not channel your anger and resentment in healthy ways, you may set up your family for domestic violence or child abuse. If your marriage or family life has been strained and you used your job as an escape, you may now be tempted to strike out. This is especially true if you had a "macho" job with heavy physical demands or even a high-powered management position.[2] You got things done by wielding power. It's common for a husband to feel impotent after losing his job, and some men may restore their sense of power by lashing out physically at weaker family members.

If you feel the urge to hit or be verbally abusive, take these steps recommended by Thomas Gordon and the National Committee for Prevention of Child Abuse:

1. Take a deep breath. And another. Then remember you are the adult.
2. Close your eyes and imagine you're hearing what your child is about to hear.
3. Press your lips together and count to ten. Or better yet, to twenty.
4. Put your child in a time-out chair. (Remember this rule: one time-out minute for each year of age.)
5. Phone a friend.
6. If someone can watch the children, go outside and take a walk.
7. Take a hot bath or splash cool water on your face.
8. Hug a pillow.
9. Turn on some music. Maybe even sing along.
10. Pick up a pencil and write down as many helpful words as you can. Save the list.

When the urge to strike passes, hug your children and let them know you love them. But if the urge doesn't pass—or the problem of family violence is heading out of control—seek professional help immediately.[3] Contact your pastor or priest, your local mental-health association, your local Family Service America organization, or your community or county department of social services.

If you or your children are victims of violence, *get out of the house*. Find a safe place—a friend or relative's house or a shelter for abused women. Seek professional help.

While some research indicates the possibility of added risk of child abuse when a wage-earner loses a job, this is still, fortunately, relatively rare. Most parents, even while in the grip of their own strong feelings, love their children and want to help them, not harm them. And many parents have found that an employment crisis can be a bittersweet time of getting to know their children in a new way.

No Energy Left for Family

Men who are employed but who hate their jobs may find that it takes so much emotional energy just to get through the work day that they have little energy left over for the family. That was true for Bob Marone, though he loves his wife and two daughters deeply. Bob suffered from depression, partly because he hated his job so much and partly because, though he tried to change fields, prospects did not look promising. What suffered even more than his time with the children was time with his wife. "So many nights I came home and sat down in the chair after the kids were put to bed, and I'd fall asleep because I just didn't have any energy. It was a major strain on our couple time," he recalled.

Not all the changes in the family will be negative. Many families reported positive changes as the result of working through a job crisis.

For some men who have been in stressful, high-pressure jobs, unemployment can bring a personality change for the better. Greg Henderson, a man in his fifties when he lost his job, said, "I've been less irritable in the last seven months of unemployment than I'd been for the last eight years. My fourteen-year-old daughter said, 'Daddy's fun when he doesn't work.'" His wife added, "Greg also did things around the house he's never done before." For the Hendersons, Greg's time without work ushered in a new and more pleasant pace of life.

Other men echoed Greg's experience. They discovered a whole new dimension of involvement with their children because they now had larger blocks of time to invest in fathering. One man told of learning the art of carpooling and developing a morning ritual of walking his children to the school bus stop. He even joined a dozen mothers for his youngest son's class trip. That day his son was the proudest kid in his class, he said, the only one whose dad came along.

Not that this period is always smooth. Fifteen-year-old Carol Falen said that it was strange to have her father ask about school, choir, and her other activities. "It was different to have to explain to him the dynamics of family life," she said. But once the initial awkwardness is over, it can be a rich time. Carol said she and her dad spent a lot of quality time together: he helped her with her homework; she helped him with home projects.

Finally, many men were pleasantly surprised to see how much help and support they received from their children. Vic and Betsey Glavach found their older children to be a tremendous help in coping with their crisis. Gigi found work cleaning houses and baby-sitting near her college campus so she wouldn't have to ask for spending money. Landy earned spending money working part time in an antique store. And when Vic had to tell fourteen-year-old Danny his parents couldn't afford to buy the equipment he needed to play hockey, he got his old go-kart and motorbike running and sold them to get the money. In another family, the eight-year-old offered to give up his allowance.

Sharing: Healthy and Unhealthy

An employment crisis can be a time for a family to pull together and for the children to help the parents accept some of the grief by sharing it. But be careful how you do this. The kids should not become too emotionally involved in the family's problem, warns New York therapist Nancy Arann. She points to one patient of hers, now in his early twenties, who still suffers the effects of his father's unemployment when he was sixteen. "His father would dump his emotional burden on him, talking to him about how hard life is and how he felt like a failure," says Arann. "[My client] felt that if only he were stronger, more powerful, he could fix things. Since he couldn't, he identified with the adult, who had failed, and was overwhelmed with despair."[4]

HOW YOUR CHILDREN MAY BE FEELING

Depending on the ages of your children and how well you handle your own emotions, your crisis may or may not affect them greatly. In fact, some kids find it a time of growth in their own faith and ability to cope. Others just enjoy seeing their fathers more.

Whatever the response, your children will react. They will pick up all the emotional tones in the family. Some children may respond by mirroring: if you're angry, they will be angry and act up. If you're depressed, they may become withdrawn. Others may try to take care of their parents, trying to be extra good to make the parents feel better. Still others may get very anxious, or they may shut down and lose their appetite or start having difficulties at school. There's no way to predict how a child will respond, says therapist Ken Potts; a lot depends on the child's personality, the family's dynamics, and where each child fits into the family.

Anxious. Children may not always understand what is going on and this will lead to anxiety. The younger child may respond to the general emotional climate; if Daddy seems down, the child may feel anxious and start acting up.

Older kids may be able to articulate their anxiety a little

more clearly. Eight-year-old Lindsey knew something was wrong when her dad came home from work and didn't reach down to give her his usual hug. He looked very sad. She grew anxious. Later on, she overheard him tell her mother that he no longer had a job. Her mother started to cry. Lindsey didn't know why losing a job was so bad, but seeing her parents so upset scared her. Lying in bed that night, she remembered that her mother once told her that the people they had seen sleeping on the sidewalks one day were there because they'd lost their jobs. When her mother came in to tuck her in, Lindsey asked tearfully, "Will we have to sleep outside in the cold because Daddy lost his job?"

A pastor recounted that a frequent question in his household when he was unemployed was, "Daddy, are we going to be poor now?" Kids also wonder if the job crisis will mean they have to move, and they may also wonder where the money will come from and feel frustrated at their inability to do anything to help.

Like adults, kids feel stress when they perceive that things are out of control. Fifteen-year-old Carol Falen said, "I didn't know what to pray for, what was going on. I didn't know if I should pray for a job or guidance for Dad. I didn't know what to say to people when they asked me what was happening."

Insecure. Most kids feel very insecure during any crisis. Children depend on their parents for stability and security. If a parent becomes very upset, it can threaten the security of that child's world.

Tom and Norma Lorner found their twelve-year-old son, Chris, becoming very angry when Tom lost his job. The surface issue was hair; he insisted on wearing it a certain way. Finally it occurred to Norma that her son was probably feeling out of control in every area of his life (the family was considering relocating), and this was his way of trying to exert some control. She gave in on the hair issue. She also mentioned to Chris and the other children that she and Tom decided not to move during the school year, so they could feel free to make friends and join the youth group. Chris relaxed after that.

Even older teenagers may feel their security threatened. Laurie Brenner, a freshman in college, suddenly saw her father in a new light, and her sense of security crumbled: "I realized my dad could be inadequate. He was just a man, subject to his weaknesses." Laurie worried that if he lost his job because of some fatal flaws, it would happen repeatedly. Then where was her security? How could she lean on him?

Teenagers and young adults often react to the insecurity they feel by getting very busy with their own activities, including jobs that will provide the money they don't feel comfortable asking for from their parents. Or they simply become more irritable. Several teenagers reported feeling annoyed that their father was around the house so much. One boy said it encroached on his sense of freedom and "space."

But the teenagers were also very resourceful in dealing with their stress. Besides getting jobs, they found other people to talk to—a youth worker, sibling, or friend. Mindy Falen gave herself reality checks: she found out that other people she knows were worried about how they were going to be able to afford college. "It helps to see others are not millionaires either. It helps to talk to others and see you're not the only one going through the money crunch."

Socially stigmatized. Though some teenagers, like Mindy, felt able to talk to friends about her situation, other teenagers may feel ashamed and stigmatized. Fifteen-year-old Carol Falen said, "A lot of my friends think it's a bad thing to be unemployed. They think there's something wrong with my dad. My friends are not Christians. Unemployment to them is people who don't want to work, who are on the street. Those kinds of pictures run through their heads, that he's weird.

They don't see the whole picture. It was hard for me to tell them that."

A father's unemployment may affect the teenager's social life as well. Carol's friends came from affluent families; they didn't understand the position she was in, she said. "If I couldn't afford to go out, I would make excuses. I tried to hide it," she said.

Carol's older sister, Mindy, was more open with her friends. "I told them I don't have any money. I told them that if they wanted me to go, they could pay for me and I would pay them back when I could. It was uncomfortable having to do that. But my friends were really understanding."

Two girls, two different experiences, no doubt because their personalities and stages of development differed. They had different worries, but they both did worry—a lot.

Worried about the future. Though younger kids may fear the future, teenagers can become obsessed with it during a job crisis. Mindy Falen worried most about going to college. "I would be lying in bed, thinking, crying, and feeling very stymied: how am I ever going to go to college?" she remembered. "What will I do with my life?"

It struck me that most teenagers I interviewed did not stop worrying even when their dads found a job. Carol Falen and Laurie Brenner were scared unemployment would happen all over again. Mindy Falen knows that the job her dad has now doesn't earn much money, so finances for college are still a major concern. It's hard to be faced with the rude realities of the work world at so young an age.

Pressured about their careers. Witnessing a parent's job crisis can profoundly affect a teenager's sense of his or her own future. Jackie Alvarez, a counselor on a rural, private college campus, is concerned about something she's noticed among college students. She calls it an insidious "trickle down" stress, which can greatly affect their academic performance and future career plans.

In an editorial in the *Chicago Tribune,* Alvarez wrote of a generation shaped by "a heavy sense of materialism" and great expectations. "The recurring message of the 1980s—that more was always better—stoked many students' expectations to great heights as they inched their way toward graduation day."[5]

Yet today's workplace is neither friendly nor fiscally solvent, and many students know it. All the teenagers I talked to said that they were thinking very carefully about their careers. Fifteen-year-old Matthew Brenner said the amount of job risk is important. He considered becoming a stock broker but jettisoned that because "It's not that stable." He wants a career that will earn him a lot of money, but job satisfaction and job security are also big factors.

Mindy Falen said, "It's real important to me to get a degree and to get it in an area that will have jobs. I want always to be able to find work." She is considering occupational therapy and nursing.

Fifteen-year-old Carol Falen also found her dad's experience has influenced how she looks at money and careers. "I think as long as I live I will be very money conscious. I'm careful how I spend my money. Also, when I start looking into careers, I will choose something that will guarantee available jobs."

Forging a realistic view of the work world and one's place in it is a major task, and it's not easy. But with some wise counsel, today's high-school and college students may form a more realistic perspective than their parents had. Ken Potts' fifteen-year-old daughter wants to major in drama, but she realizes that the chances of becoming a famous actress are slim. So she's planning to make drama her avocation and to find something in business that will match her interests. "I applauded her for her thinking," said Ken, "even though a part of me wants to tell her, 'You can do and be whatever you want.' That's just not as realistic."

Closer Bonds

Many of the older children I interviewed told me their family is closer after they together struggled through a job crisis. The Falen sisters said that the family always eats dinner together. "Afterward we talk and talk and laugh and have devotions. Laughing a lot keeps me sane," said Mindy.

Carol Falen observed that the family learned to look at the positive things in a situation. She pointed out, insightfully, that before the job crisis, when everything was basically positive in their lives, they tended to focus on the negative, whatever didn't fit the smooth norm. Now that the "norm" is somewhat stressful, the positive things stand out as real gifts of grace.

Mindy said she learned a lot about her dad during the eight months he was unemployed—including how much like him she is! The Falen girls believe the job crisis cemented them as a family. Carol said, "Before, we were all on different wavelengths because we never had any kind of real worry. Now we're more aware of how we each act and react. This has made us more aware of the fact that we are a family."

These bonds were strengthened primarily because the Falens worked to keep the communication lines open. This is crucial because often what a child imagines is wrong is far worse than the reality. Also, children often assume that family problems are their fault. Most important, as one woman pointed out, if we shield our children from our struggles, how will they see God at work?

They will see God at work as they see you draw upon your own faith, lean on God for strength, and look to others for help. Modeling these coping skills for handling life's tough problems may be one of the greatest gifts you can give to your children.

· 6 ·

Help Your Children Cope

How you as parents handle the job situation strongly influences how your children will cope. Laurie Brenner said her father usually kept his spirits up, but her mother was obviously stressed during the first two periods of her father's unemployment. That led to stress for Laurie. She felt her mother sought to control her children to compensate for the lack of control she felt. Laurie was probably right. But when her mother was more at peace during the third and latest period of unemployment, Laurie also found it easier to handle.

Mothers have a unique responsibility to help their children keep a positive perspective. Children often reflect the mother's attitude toward the father. Men need to feel honored, accepted, and loved for who they are, not for just what they do. A job crisis is a real testing ground for demonstrating this honor. The wife can do so much to influence, for better or worse, how the children perceive their father.

One of the biggest challenges of a job crisis is to allow yourselves to redefine what being a man, including being a father, is all about. Marian Henriquez Nuedel, an attorney in Chicago, suggests, "Such a redefinition has to be sufficiently serious that a man who spends all his waking hours out of the home earning money—no matter how much—will be viewed by himself and everybody else as a failed father, while a man who can't find a job, but renovates the family's dwelling and teaches his children the skills necessary to clean, plaster, paint, and build, tends his babies, helps his children learn to read, and gives them a sense of moral worth, will be esteemed by himself and others as a thoroughly successful father."[1]

If the success issue is a struggle for you—either as an unemployed husband or as a wife—do all you possibly can to reorient your thinking about what it means to be a man and a father. Your children are daily being molded by your image of what a true man is. You may say all the right things, but if your inner attitude is that something is wrong with an unemployed man, the kids will pick up on that.

WHAT TO TELL YOUR CHILDREN

If you haven't already told your children what's going on, you and your spouse should sit down and decide just what to say. Again, different children will respond differently. But most children are sensitive to changes within the family and will sense something is different. You need to keep the lines of communication open so that your children understand what's happening and how it affects them.

Allay Their Fears

Your children may fear the worst. You can allay their fears in several ways:

Always tell the truth. This doesn't mean going into the gory details; you can sugar-coat the truth for young children. But don't pretend nothing is wrong or make up another explanation like, "Everything's okay. Daddy's taking a vacation." Children usually know that something is wrong. If you are not honest with them, they will create their own explanations, which can cause more stress than the real reason for the family's current problems.

Let your children know the facts, but communicate them in a calm, confident way. "Daddy's lost his job, but he's working hard at finding a new one."

Communicate your sense of mastery. Let your children know what is the worst possible thing that could happen—and then point out that in all likelihood it won't happen. When you say, "Even if we lose this house, we'll always have a place to sleep," you will communicate your confidence that you will all survive even the worst thing that can happen.

"Inoculate" them from your stress. Tell your children that you both may have less patience because it's hard to look for another job. As a result, you may lose your temper more easily or may be more crabby. Assure them that your crabbiness is no reflection of how you feel about them. It's just part of the process of finding another job. That way when you do lose your temper, your children will say to themselves, *Oh, they told me they'd get like this. I'm not worried.*

What to Say to the Children

The younger the child, the less you have to say and the more you have to work at providing a stable emotional environment. This may mean asking for help from friends and family to take care of the children for a few hours so you and your spouse have some relief and time to concentrate on the practical issues of the job search.

Children as young as preschool age will sense something is wrong, so do explain in terms they can understand what is going on. Child psychiatrist Dr. Marlene Schmidt suggests that you be sure to emphasize that the problem happened, that they did not cause it in any way, and that you, the parents, are responsible for fixing it and will take care of it.[2]

You can tailor the following information to your child's age: "Daddy's a little sad now because he has to find a new job. Sometimes he might even seem a little angry, but it's not because of you. Don't worry. He'll be okay and so will you. He's going to find a new job soon, and then he'll have a place to go to work."

Because security is an issue for most age groups, assure them that things won't change much. You can tailor the following information to your child's age: "Daddy lost his job. He is a little sad because he liked his work and liked earning money. He's going to be looking for a new job, and he'll probably find something even better. In the meantime, things will go on pretty much the same. You'll go to school and play with your friends and do all the things you usually do."[3]

Older children (between ten and eighteen) are better able to understand the problems associated with the loss of a job. As we discussed earlier, they also look to the future more and will personally feel the economic changes. Your teenager's quest for identity often translates into some basic material expressions: cars, cosmetics, music, clothes, food, clothes, dates, clothes, entertainment, and clothes.[4]

Communicate to the preadolescent all the things mentioned above, adding something like, "We are going to have to be a little more careful about how we spend our money for a while. Instead of going to the movies this weekend, we'll rent a special video and make our own popcorn. But otherwise, things won't change too much."

Teenagers will have more questions. You'll need to level with them. Acknowledge that they may feel the stigma from their peers. You might say something like, "You know, some of your friends might not understand, and they might tease you about it. Think you can handle that?" In most cases, they will be able to handle it. They'll also know you understand what they may be going through. You might even suggest they tell their peers, "My dad is looking real hard for a job, and he wants the best job he can find." This is more positive than saying, "My dad's out of work."

Talk over anything else that may affect your teenager's future. Discuss college options, such as attending a less expensive public college for a couple of years or working to save some money. They may respond with anger, which is natural, but their anger can also induce guilt in you. Acknowledge that you know this is rough on them, but if you all work together, each doing what he or she can, you will weather this, and everything will be okay.

Keep the lines of communication open. Say, "This is how Dad is feeling. How is it for you?" Accept their feelings, and help them to try to see that you can work together on solutions. Carol Falen said, "A lot of times my fears were because I didn't know what was going on. Sometimes talking to Mom helped me to understand what was happening. When I got the bigger picture, that helped me deal with it better."

But sometimes Alice Falen, Carol's mom, didn't have any answers either. Carol said, "Sometimes I would go to her and say I don't have enough money for this, and I have to have this by this time—and we cried together."

Carol Falen also found much relief in talking to her youth pastor's wife. Recognize that your teenager may feel uncomfortable talking to you about the job crisis. In that case, you might want to suggest that he or she turn to another responsible adult, such as a counselor, a church friend, a scout-troop leader, a teacher, or school counselor.

LEARN TO SURVIVE—EVEN THRIVE —AS A FAMILY

In addition to maintaining effective communication, you can do several other things to fulfill your promises to keep things normal and weather this storm as a family.

Don't Create a False Sense of Reality

It's hard to hear your child say, "Daddy, are we poor now?" In an effort to prove that the answer is no, you may be tempted to shower your children with new toys and treats. Resist the impulse. It only creates a false sense of reality that can confuse young children. They can see that you are upset about money, so they will wonder, "Why are they still buying us presents?" They begin questioning their own ability to understand reality and their parents' truthfulness. Creating such a contradictory situation also sends the message that it's fine to pretend things are okay when they aren't. To avoid this pitfall, remind yourselves that children are better off when they know about the family crisis and are encouraged to participate, in an age-appropriate way, in dealing with it.[5]

Let the Kids Help Out

One of the potential positive results of a job crisis is that children can learn problem-solving skills through watching their parents and through participating themselves in solving the problem. Dr. Antoinette Saunders, founder of the Chicago-based The Capable Kid counseling centers, suggests creating a chart on which each child lists the way he or she helped out in a given week. Next to the four- or five-year-old's name, for instance, might be "played quietly while Daddy was on the phone" or "brushed my teeth by myself while Mommy was writing letters." A seven-year-old's contribution might be "helped clear the table after dinner every night," while an eleven-year-old "helped get the baby ready for bed so Dad could have more time to send out résumés."

Another tactic to get your kids involved without over-burdening them is to make a game out of problem solving. You can say, "You know, since I lost my job, we have to make our money last longer. So let's make up a list of ways we can have fun without spending much money." Such a list might include things like riding bikes, playing games at home, visiting a favorite relative or friend, or preparing a special family meal. You can also take your children grocery shopping and let them help you figure out ways to stretch the budget. Boxes of macaroni and cheese and jars of peanut butter are not only cheap, but kids often prefer them over potatoes au gratin.

Don't Overburden Your Child

While it's appropriate to let your child help, always make it clear that this is primarily your problem to solve. Kids will naturally want to help, and they don't have a clear sense of boundaries. One nine-year-old boy began dancing on the street for money; he thought the money he brought in would cheer up his unemployed father. As touching as his gesture might be, it's a warning sign that the child is trying to be the parent's caregiver. Those roles should never be reversed.

If it seems as if a child is taking on too much responsibility for making things better, tell him or her firmly, "I know I've been feeling bad and that you want to help. I really appreciate it and love you for it. But sometimes people have to feel sad for a while. I'll feel fine again soon. The most important thing for you to remember is that I'll always be able to take care of you. You don't ever have to worry about that. I love you very much, and it makes me feel good just to know you love me, too."[6]

Maintain a Normal Routine

Routine and predictability assure children that their world is safe. The more you can keep their daily routines the same, the less they'll feel the upheaval. If you have to pare back, as much as possible trim the things that won't affect their daily lives. Cut out the big vacation rather than the weekly piano lessons. Cut out the cleaning help rather than the child's regular baby-sitter.

Make an effort to keep meal, bed, bath, and play times on the same schedule as always. Even if you don't feel like it, if you've always read a bedtime story, continue to do so. Your children will suffer more from a disrupted routine than from your temporary inability to buy them any special toys or goodies.[7]

Ease Any Necessary Transitions

If your job search drags on, you may be forced to make some adjustments in your child's routine. If so, prepare your child for any changes you'll have to make.

For instance, an extended period of unemployment may force you to take your eight-year-old out of private school and put her into public school. If you can, do it at the beginning of a new term, when the transition will be more natural. Explain to your child what is going to happen. Say, "I've found a wonderful new school I would like you to try. I've met the teacher, and she is very nice. The children seem like a lot of fun too. Tomorrow, we'll go over to see the new school, and you can meet the teacher."

Then take the child over to the school, introduce her to the teacher, and, if possible, spend an hour or two there. Also, explain what will be different about her routine—who will take her to school, how she'll get home, where she'll eat her lunch. Be sure to answer her questions as honestly and simply as possible.

Keep Your Emotions Under Control

Nothing disturbs a child more than seeing a parent who is emotionally out of control. It's perfectly appropriate to let your child see that you are sad because you or your spouse lost your job—that's only natural. But crying and ranting about the raw deal you got should be reserved for times when your children are safely out of earshot. Otherwise, you'll threaten your children's confidence in your ability to take care of them. This holds true both for the job seeker and his wife. As the spouse, you need to avoid mirroring your husband's stress because your kids will be looking to you for reassurance that their world is still safe. If you're nervous or distraught and you convey that to the kids, they will think, *I guess things really are bad if both Mom and Dad are this worried.*

Also be sure to deal with your anger in places away from the children. Realize that you will be tempted to take it out on the kids, and find another way to vent your pain. Go out for a long walk and talk to your spouse; call a friend; find a support group; seek therapy, if necessary; throw your energy into an exhaustive job hunt. But don't let your kids bear the brunt of your rage.

Seek Outside Help, If Necessary

Job loss and the stress it causes can throw a family into turmoil, despite your best efforts to cope. If you find yourself losing control too often, seek help. And if your children start to experience problems as a result of your job stress, you may need to seek professional help for them. Regressive behavior such as clinginess, withdrawing from friends, loss of appetite, disturbed sleep, a sudden drop in grades at school, a return to former habits such as bedwetting, or an increase in behavioral problems in school may be signs that your child is having trouble coping.

If your children are mature enough, try talking with them about how they're feeling. Spending a little extra "quality time" with them may also help. But if the worrisome behavior persists for more than a few weeks, you should seek outside help. Your children's pediatrician can help you find a qualified mental-health professional.

Hold Family Meetings

Meeting together as a family is one of the best ways to keep the lines of communication open and emphasize the importance of pulling together as a family. The Falens did this, and the girls thought the meetings were very helpful because it gave everyone a chance to speak his or her mind and share the burden.

During a family meeting, the father can offer an update on his job hunt. (If things aren't going well, though, skip the details. You don't want to add to the children's anxiety. A simple, "I could use prayer for some encouragement and some better leads" should do it.) Then, each family member can express what's been hard about this time and what's been fun about it. Having to postpone buying those new sneakers was hard, but having Dad at home to play basketball after school was great. This is also a good opportunity for you as parents to remind your children of the contribution they've made. Simply say, "You know, Carla, your washing the cars this week really freed up time for me to put into the job hunt. I called someone who had a good lead for me. You were really a big help."

These meetings should be held every week on the same night. Pick a night, perhaps a Sunday, when the pace is slower and everyone has a chance to regroup and prepare for the week ahead. It should be a time when the kids can have your undivided attention, which is especially important during a stressful period.

Take Time to Have Fun as a Family

Whatever you can do to boost your own spirits as parents will also make the kids happier, and their happiness then cheers you up further. Maintain a family routine, exercise regularly, eat a low-fat, high-carbohydrate diet, spend time with positive people. Spend time with the kids, doing fun things that are inexpensive. Twenty-year-old Laurie Brenner, looking back on her family's periods of unemployment, advises parents regularly "to make it a point to forget about the problems and just be a family."

Kay and Larry Strom decided that despite the fact that Larry was out of a job, they would make the summer special for the family. They made a list of free activities they could do. They determined to use the summer to cement their family and make lifelong memories in the hope that their ten- and twelve-year-old children would forget the endless meals of rice and beans and squash from the garden and remember instead the summer they made sand castles at the beach and visited every museum in town.[8]

Pray for Your Children

Praying regularly for your children may be the best thing you can do for them. A job crisis can be a time when they turn to God and make their faith their own, as Carol Falen did. "I learned you can't just cut off communication with God," she said. "Before my dad lost his job, devotions weren't high on my list of priorities. I realized then I needed to concentrate on the Word and make my faith my own. I learned God is constantly there. The more I learned about him, the more confident I was." Her sister, Mindy, learned, "You can't do things by yourself. You have to trust God to lay out the steppingstones. He knows what he is doing and has a plan and purpose for everything."

Part of trusting God in this crisis is trusting that he will accomplish his purposes in your family as well. When you're in the midst of the crisis, you can't always see a purpose. But those who have been through the crisis and come out on the other side have looked back and have seen many good things happen in themselves and their families. Carol Falen said she learned, "No matter what happens, my family will always be there. Also, God will always provide for us."

Laurie Brenner, a college freshman when I talked to her, reflected on the lessons she's learned: "I've grown a lot as a person and in my faith in Jesus. I value people and life a lot more now. You realize life is so fleeting, and you can't trust in things—that isn't all bad." She has also seen God provide, and she has seen her mother grow from an overcontrolling, anxious person to a wife who has faith in God and in her husband. I couldn't help feeling Laurie learned as much about God's power through seeing her parents' faith and the results as she did from her grandmother's offer to pay for her schooling and her father's experience in always finding another job by fall.

Pulling together as a family will require resources from outside yourself: support of extended family and friends as well as material and spiritual resources. Before you can draw on the help that's available, you may need to work through some barriers first. But it is possible for you and your children to come through your crisis with a deeper sense of what it means to be a family, dependent on each other and totally dependent on God.

· 7 ·

What to Tell
Other People

U nemployment is the great equalizer," said one man who had experienced unemployment several times. What he meant was that it doesn't matter who you are or what job you once had—if you once earned $200,000 and are now earning nothing, you are in the same boat with the person who once earned $20,000 and is now earning nothing.

A scene at the unemployment office makes the same point. As Barry Crull described it, "You have people who are dressed in rags, and you have people who are dressed up in designer suits and everything in between." Laborers, bankers, salespeople, teachers—all stand in the same line because they face the same situation: they are out of a job.

If unemployment pulls its sufferers into the same boat, it also casts its passengers on a lonely voyage that often isolates them from others. In some ways unemployment is the unfair unequalizer: though you still have the same skills, suddenly you are no longer on par with other machinists or bankers or realtors or salespeople. No matter what you were doing before, no matter how prestigious or respectable your former job was, suddenly you are stripped of that social status; your elevator is now on the bottom floor. You may find some part-time or even full-time work to put food on the table, but if it's not in your field, you will still feel stuck on that bottom floor. You can't shake your doubts about why you were the one chosen to get the ax, and you can't get over the feeling that other people secretly wonder the same thing.

WHY COUPLES HIDE OUT

When it comes to admitting the fact that they are not fully employed, some couples can be as evasive as a politician. Why do we hide the truth?

Fear of Other People's Reactions

Fear of other people's reactions may cause us to hide the problem in the first place. Remember Derek and Karen Halstad? Derek was so preoccupied with what others thought that he constructed an elaborate system of denial to cover up their true situation. Though most people do not go as far as Derek and Karen did, many will go months before they tell family members or friends. For almost two years Michael Catlin could not bring himself to tell his dad or his brother he was out of work. Finally, he did tell his dad, but he made it sound as if he had just lost his job. His dad's reaction surprised him. "He was supportive," Michael said. "He said, 'Well, those things happen, and I know that you try your best.' But he never asked us if we needed any money, and he never gave the father-son hug of support, but we didn't expect that of him. Our relationship did open up a little more after I told him."

Michael's experience points to two things other people also have experienced. First, families sometimes surprise us and are more supportive than we think they'll be. But second, they also may not come through for us in the way we secretly hope they might. I repeatedly heard couples express disappointment in what their family members *didn't* do. We hide the truth from our extended family because we fear we will get the kind of response we don't want, whether that means a total lack of understanding or simply not doing as much to help as we would like them to do.

Bad Experiences

Sometimes our fears are based on reality. Some people *won't* understand. Family members can be insensitive, even cruel. Derek's grandmother once said to Karen, "Derek should go out and get a job, any job." Karen's father would bad-mouth Derek to Karen.

Friends also can make us feel as if something is wrong with us. Mitch had to give up teaching when he lost his voice because of a recurring medical problem. For months he searched for something else. "Sometimes," Mitch said, "people would ask Pam, 'Has your husband found a job yet?' [When she said I hadn't], I got the feeling that the person was thinking, 'Oh, why not? What's wrong with him?'"

A job crisis fosters loneliness, especially for the men. The images of maleness are deeply imbedded in our culture: pioneer, cowboy, farmer, detective, astronaut. Archetypes mirror the desire to stand proudly alone, never needing anything, never depending on anyone. Needing is seen as a sign of inadequacy, not strength. Because of this, men often shoulder their problems alone. They don't know how to reach out to other men; they're not sure how to ask for or offer help because then they may be perceived as violating this male norm. Brett Parrish does not have anyone with whom he can share candidly what it feels like to be in his situation. In fact, he felt almost deliberately cut off: "I had developed relationships with people on the board of directors of the organization that terminated my job, but I never heard from them. No one calls. It appears that people avoid me."

The wife of the unemployed man also is caught up in the loneliness. If her husband is not open about his job situation, she faces a cruel dilemma: either be honest with other people and go against her husband (feeling as if she's betraying him), or go along with the ruse and cut herself off from support. But she too feels the stigma and may find herself withdrawing regardless of her husband's reactions.

Brett's wife, Mona, found herself withdrawing from people. "You feel as if you're wearing a scarlet 'U.' In our circle not many people are unemployed. It's hard to be around people, hard to be in groups of people who have a normal lifestyle. People forget, and they ask, 'Where did you go on vacation?' Or they get tired of hearing about your problems."

Martha and Michael Catlin, feeling their marriage was stretched to the breaking point after almost a year of unemployment, felt desperate for some outside support. They opened up to their Sunday school class, asking for prayer that Martha would be able to put up with Michael's mood swings and depression. After the class someone told them they should not have "aired their laundry in public." They should have shared with only a few people, in private, they were told.

The rebuke cut deeply. It said to them, "You can't admit failure or weakness around us." The Catlins returned to their isolation, struggling alone with their issues of self-esteem and respect, anger and disappointment. And now to that was added new anger and disappointment in people who should have supported them in their time of need.

People can be insensitive, but try to remember that their insensitivity reflects more about them than it does about you.

WHY SOME PEOPLE WITHDRAW

Not everyone will be supportive and understanding during your job crisis. Many people simply don't deal well with bad news, and they may be uncomfortable with your situation. A friend's or a relative's job loss may threaten other people. Or they themselves may have suffered through an employment crisis. News of your situation might elicit memories a person would rather not resurrect.

Another reason people may start withdrawing is to protect themselves from the pain of separation if it appears you may have to relocate. Or you may be the one to back away for the same reason. The Lorners started to withdraw from their friends when it looked as if they would have to move. They also sensed their friends withdrawing for the same reason.

For other people, news of a job loss touches a deep fear. Psychologists report increases of people suffering from panic attacks related to job loss. Dr. Donald Dossey, founder and director of the Phobia Institute of West Los Angeles and Stress Management Centers of Southern California, says that during a recent wave of recession, he was seeing weekly twenty-five or thirty patients who said they suffer from anxieties over unemployment and losing everything. "It's a big thing right now," Dossey said. "People are afraid of losing their jobs, being kicked out of their homes, the whole bit."[1]

Some people just don't want to be reminded that next week they could be in your shoes. Rather than admit this to themselves, they may subconsciously decide you must have brought it on yourself somehow. Or maybe they fear that if they hang around you, whatever caused you to lose your job will spread to them. Martha Catlin said at times she felt "quarantined, as if I had the chicken pox and other people felt they shouldn't get too close lest our 'disease' be contagious."

On the other hand, George Talman found that the fear of losing their own jobs made some people *more supportive* rather than distant. George felt that the concern of the men in his Bible study group stemmed from their fear that they could be in George's shoes. Their thinking was probably more like, "If

I'm there for this guy, maybe others will be there if and when I need it."

Friends and family also react according to how we present ourselves. If we don't want to "burden them," we may be the ones doing the abandoning. Or if we feel ashamed, others will sense our shame and back off. That's because, according to Dr. Gershen Kaufman, "Human beings innately resist the lowering of the head or eyes in shame." If you feel shame or if you communicate shame, people move away because they are so uncomfortable with shame. Dr. Kaufman points out, "In this culture, people are not encouraged to reveal their failings and inferiorities. They are not taught in the school or family how to tolerate shame, effectively release it, and overcome its sources."[2] Rather than face your shame, people may back away.

Our attitude affects how others respond. One former long-term friend of an out-of-work executive said, "I got so tired of listening to that guy tell me about his troubles. All he did was . . . gripe about what a raw deal he got. I couldn't see that he was doing one constructive thing to get his life back together. So I just quit returning his phone calls and avoided places where I thought I might bump into him."[3] People with little capacity for compassion will avoid you if they perceive you as being "too negative."

It would help if people could be as understanding as we need them to be at times. But unfortunately, most people are simply too preoccupied with their own lives to stop and think about how we might be feeling. For them, life moves on in busyness and demands, achievements and rewards, while we're left behind, trailing in the dust.

Sometimes we may feel disappointed in others because, consciously or unconsciously, we expect them to help us more than they do. "Why don't my parents offer to pay for the kids' school clothes?" or whatever. Many of the people I talked to admitted to having such expectations of family or friends or fellow Christians. Michael Catlin said, "I threw out the rope to people I thought should help [those in his Sunday school class]. I wanted to trust them with some of the responsibility for our spiritual well-being."

I have found that if we expect friends or family members to find us a job or bail us out of a financial dilemma, we're expecting too much. It's much easier emotionally to accept any help as a gift but not to expect it. As we assume responsibility for our welfare while at the same time we trust God, other people are free to follow their hearts, and they often respond in generosity. However, if we have expectations of people, however unvoiced, they may sense those expectations and resist. I think it's best to bring our expectations in line with what we know to be true of human nature.

Accept the fact that some people will react inappropriately or ineffectively. But don't let such awkward reactions stop you from talking to people in your network. The stakes are too high for you to hide behind the smoke screen of "everything's all right."

THE DANGERS OF HIDING THE TRUTH

One danger in trying to hide the truth is that we lose touch with reality. As Karen Halstad said, "When the smoke screen is up for so long, it's hard to be honest with your spouse, or even with yourself." Keeping up a façade drains energy that you badly need for coping.

In time, the ploy of secrecy will backfire. The only family member Derek Halstad told about his joblessness was his mother. But eventually he grew resentful because he knew other people must have known what was going on, at least to some degree. Yet no one seemed to care. He felt judged and misjudged. And Karen felt a deep internal conflict. "Most of me agreed with other people, that Derek was not being fair to his family. He should take just any job. But part of me was always on his side. Part of me supported him finding a job he could love."

Laura Joiner, whose husband, John, could not find a job after finishing his Ph.D., recalled times he would be on the phone talking to his father as if he had the best job in the world. She would think, "Who is he talking about?" Since John was denying the reality of their situation, Laura didn't feel as if she could openly confront the issue or air her feelings, inside or outside the family. If children are involved in a situation like this, denial and secrecy can lead to dysfunctional patterns of coping with reality.

Couples caught in denial begin a dangerous downward spiral. A major part of a man's identity is tied up in his job. But identity is also connected to relationships. If a man lacks a work identity and compounds this lack by cutting off his relationships, he's doubly impoverished. He will tend either to lean more on his wife for a sense of who he is or to pull away from even her. His wife may try doubly hard to be supportive, often in spite of her own doubts and fears. These dynamics strain some marriages to the breaking point. No one relationship can carry all that weight. I talked to one couple who did withdraw and hide behind the smoke screen. Today the husband is trying to divorce the wife, and they are carrying deep heartaches.

The stress may also lead to health problems in either or both spouses, impeding the job search. Susan Gore of the University of Michigan Institute for Social Research found that men who had relatively little support for their situation from their wives, friends, and relatives and who did not feel they had many opportunities to be sociable had more health symptoms and days of illness, higher cholesterol levels, more ulcer activity, poorer economic recovery, and more depression and self-blame than did men with adequate social support.[4]

Helen Hosier, in her book *Suddenly Unemployed,* tells of a

husband and wife who had both lost their jobs. They couldn't bring themselves to share their misfortune with anyone, not even family members. It was not until they were evicted from their home that family and neighbors knew there was a problem.

As Karen Henderson said so pointedly, "How can anyone support you if they don't know you have a problem?"

Her husband, Greg, added, "How can you put together a network if you're still pretending you're employed?"

Telling people is crucial. But it only makes sense, in the light of what we've said about how some people react, to be selective about whom you tell.

TEAR DOWN THE SMOKE SCREEN

Pastor and writer Steve Brown once said, "The way to find out who your real friends are is either to succeed or fail." Some people will stand by you. Most of the time, it will be the people you already know and trust. One husband and wife said that during their job crisis they deepened a few relationships rather than scattering their efforts. They spent lots of time with another couple in a similar situation.

Decide What to Say to Whom

It's natural to want to withdraw and not let anyone in on your real struggles. But you must work to counteract that tendency. The first step is to talk with your spouse and decide not only whom you will tell but also what you will tell each person. As you look for people with whom you can be honest and open, consider these questions.

- How close are you to these people? If you have already built a relationship of trust, you can probably trust them with the details of your job crisis. If they are perceptive people, they may be able to ask you some of the hard questions without making you feel defensive or uneasy.

- Have these people proven themselves to be sensitive and empathetic in the past? The Lorners knew whom to reach out to during Tom's job crisis because they had already swallowed their pride and asked for help when Norma had a major surgery a couple of years earlier. The Lorners knew that they could trust these people to listen carefully and respond with sensitivity.

- What kind of bond is between you, and how strong is that bond? The bond may be parenting children of the same ages or being in the same Bible study group or growing up together. The stronger the bond, obviously, the stronger the chance they will be able to be helpful and supportive.

- What might you need from these people, either now or later? I'm not suggesting that you use people; I'm assuming you already have some kind of relationship. You may need help from a colleague in finding job leads. You may need to brainstorm with someone who is in a field you've thought of trying. You may need to have weekly talking times with a couple who has been through unemployment before.

- What might possibly get in the way in your relationship? For example, if your friends have more money than they need and you often socialized at a restaurant, it would be difficult to continue that. Or if your family never did like your spouse and this new development will just give them more ammunition, it might be best to keep a low profile.

One spouse may be more comfortable with openness than the other may be. Talk this over frankly with each other. Reaffirm your trust in each other. Bob Marone knew that Kerry talked to her female friends about their situation, but he trusted that she would not violate their privacy or make him look bad. And Kerry upheld that trust. When she talked to friends, it was about her feelings more than about Bob. It's crucial that both spouses keep this trust sacred. Without it, the marriage can be destroyed.

Karen and Derek Halstad never did resolve their tensions over how open to be. Karen finally cracked one day and told her sister. Then she told others the truth. But Derek never could be that open, and he resented that Karen had torn down his façade. She, in turn, bitterly resented him for trying to hide the truth and expecting her to lie. It got to the point where Derek hated being around her friends because he felt they knew things he didn't want them to know. The trust had been broken.

Prepare for Possible Negative Reactions

Decide ahead of time to let insensitive comments roll off your back. Or picture them going in one ear and right out the other without getting stuck in between. Remind yourself that the reactions of others, positive or negative, probably say more about their character than about yours.

Re-evaluate Social Situations

Decide ahead of time how you want to respond to *The Question*. Bob Marone felt ill at ease at social events, particularly those related to Kerry's workplace. "You're surrounded by people who are professionals and pulling in a good salary, and they say, 'Well, what do you do?' And responding that you're looking around for work or between jobs—I mean, it's certainly not a badge to be worn on the outside of the coat." So he just didn't attend those functions.

Other people find social occasions to be good times to develop a network. Bob Brenner took this tack. He told everyone and anyone that he was looking for a job in the flexible packaging business. It was hard on his pride, but his need to find a new job overcame his pride. He said he found other people very open and supportive.

Jack and Marita Wilson found themselves in a quandary because most of their friends were related to Jack's workplace. When Jack was laid off, suddenly those relationships were strained. The couple thought that their friends felt torn between their loyalty to their employer and their friendship with them. So Jack and Marita finally decided to avoid parties and gatherings with some of his former colleagues for a while. It was just too difficult to spend time with them, wondering if their friends were thinking, "Why him and not me?" Though Jack still felt able to call on these important business contacts for help during his job search, he and Marita felt more comfortable keeping those relationships at a distance.

You may lose a few friendships in the process, but work hard to maintain at least a professional relationship with people who can help with your spouse's career plans or your own. Many of these relationships will be important to your network of contacts as you look for a new position.

Continue to Socialize

Try to find ways within your means to maintain some kind of social life. For example, take advantage of free concerts, free days at museums, a day at the beach, inexpensive church activities. And invite another family or couple along. Invite friends over for game night at your house. Keeping up some kind of social life, when you can just relax and enjoy non-stressful activity, will make you feel more normal. And it will allow others to relate to you in more normal ways as well.

Find a Support Group

Even as you work to retain normalcy, you have to recognize the special needs and stresses you have right now. You need others who can speak to those needs and help carry the load. Each person is different. Some people get enough support from one or two close friends; other people need to feel part of something larger, and a group best fits them. Some people prefer to seek their support in groups they're already part of; George Talman found his support in the men's Bible study he had attended. Craig, on the other hand, felt more comfortable spending time with other people who were going through the same thing, others who had no preconceived idea of who he was. He joined a support group sponsored by several churches in his area. (Chapter 12 gives details on how to find or start such a group.)

Whoever your support team turns out to be, choose people with whom you can be frank. You can say, "I'm feeling a little discouraged these days; please pray for me."

Let People Know Your Needs

If someone asks if you need anything and you believe they're sincere, don't lie and say no. You can say, "I'm a little worried about how we're going to pay for school supplies." Norma Lorner came to believe that she was doing herself and others a service by verbalizing her needs. She was growing in her ability to receive, and she was allowing others to grow in their ability to give.

Other people found that when they let their needs be known, others responded with surprising generosity. You may be amazed at how many people will be glad and honored when you are open with them. Most of us do feel honored when someone trusts us with a need. We back away if we feel the person wants to use us, but we're more than willing to help if people just need a hand to help them over a rough spot in their lives.

Take the Risk

It will feel risky to be open with other people. But I urge you to do it, selectively as I've said. In fact, if you have to err on one side or the other, I think it's best to err on the side of being too open. Yes, you may get hurt. But too many people have told me they expected rejection and received only support. Many older men would not even consent to an interview with me, I assume because it was too painful for them to discuss their situation. Yet other men of that same generation who were open said they found that people were more supportive than they had thought they would be. My own husband realized that, hard as it was, sharing his problem was a step toward overcoming it. Not keeping it to himself was a step toward relationships and away from isolation. It allowed him to receive whatever encouragement others had to offer—which was more than he had dreamed.

We miss so much if we're not open with others, especially with others from a caring church. One husband and wife who were open and let the local body of believers reach out to them were told later that the whole church benefited from watching their faith and stretching to reach out and care for them. "Because of Bob's willingness to share his job loss," Gail said, "we were an example that showed the body how it was supposed to work, being entwined with each other's lives."

Some people may fail you. But you can survive that. What you may not survive is cutting yourself off from those who are able and willing to hold out the life preserver of friendship and caring.

· 8 ·

Recast the
American Dream

Roberta Schaefer never dreamed she would be permanently in the low-income bracket when she married her husband, Kyle, who had a master's degree. The kind of work Kyle loves to do—writing, especially movie-script writing—yields an uncertain income. He tried other things like selling life insurance and starting his own business, but none of them succeeded. His choice seems limited to continuing at something he loves, even though the job pays very little, or working at a job that pays better, even though he hates the job.

Kyle has opted to follow his dream, and Roberta supports him, mostly because, as she said, "I know how miserable he is when he works at something he hates." But the tradeoff for the Schaefers has been giving up the American Dream of upward mobility and learning some hard lessons in thrift along the way.

Many more people are having to give up the same things and learn the same hard lessons, but they feel they have no choice. For millions of Americans, the American Dream of upward mobility is vanishing.

THE VANISHING DREAM

Loretta and Mark Tryer and their two children enjoyed the economic boom of the 1980s in New England. Loretta stayed home on Cape Cod raising two boys, while Mark earned almost $35,000 doing carpentry and piloting boats. Then the recession hit, and Mark worked odd jobs. The family had to move in with his mother, and Loretta became the main wage-earner. She worked in a hospital food-service department for about sixteen hours a week—a job that paid well by local standards. She hoped it would lead to a full-time position, which would provide the health insurance her family didn't have. She is also considering going back to school to train as a nurse or physician's assistant. "I don't feel that my future is all gloom and doom," Loretta said.[1]

But she is also realistic. "About a year ago, we were sitting around the table, and my mother said, 'I feel sorry for you. Your children probably won't have as good a life as you did growing up, and that's going to be hard for you to face,'" Loretta recalled. "I thought about it, and I said, 'You're right.'"[2]

This is a turbulent time for our economy. Corporations continue their policies of downsizing to compete in a global economy. Many of these jobs were in middle-management, the traditional route to upward mobility. "Today's global economy is reserving its richest rewards for the well-educated or for those working in jobs sheltered from foreign competition. The result is that millions of workers in the bottom one half to three quarters of America's labor force are butting up against a ceiling. They are doing worse than they once did and working harder than ever while falling behind the better-off."[3]

Manufacturing jobs are fast being displaced by robots, so that millions of people find themselves in the ranks of the "structurally unemployed"—people whose jobs are made obsolete because of technology. And because new belt-tightening measures have taken place in most American work-places in the 1990s, it's harder and harder to earn a salary that will pay as much as it did five or six years ago. The result is that "upward mobility is becoming a vanishing dream for many," according to Robert Reich, author of *The Work of Nations*. In fact, downward mobility is turning into a way of life for many people.

The United States now includes 33.6 million people who live below the poverty line (a four-person family that earns less than $13,921 annually). Two million of these people dropped to the poverty level in 1990 alone.[4] Nearly one out of every five workers in the United States is working part time; many of them would rather have full-time work. The average part-time worker earns only 60 percent as much per hour as a full-time worker, and the part-time worker is less likely to have medical or pension benefits.

Add to all this the growing tax bite, and it's clear that for many of us, living on our income will become increasingly more difficult. At least it's discouraging to me to know that for every dollar of income I need, I must earn almost twice that to take care of taxes (I pay double social security, since I'm self-employed). Though Gene and I both now have jobs, neither job pays all that well. We still scramble to make ends meet.

I don't mean to depress you with all these numbers. You do have something to do with whether your downward mobility is temporary or permanent, as we'll see in chapter 10. But if you're in the midst of an employment crisis—either because you're unemployed or because you're underemployed—by definition you're not employed at the level you want. And that takes some emotional adjustment. It takes rethinking our expectations of life and work.

RETHINKING THE AMERICAN DREAM

You probably have grown up expecting to have a brighter future than your parents had. For generations, this American Dream seemed almost to be a birthright. And for several decades, the American economy has largely delivered. Now that we are in a turbulent time of change, many of us are caught in the middle: we cling to our old expectations and dreams while we fight a growing fear that maybe things won't work out that way after all, for us or for our children. As Tom Morton put it, "I studied hard. I worked hard. I prayed. I paid my dues. What more does anyone want? This is the American Dream we're talking about, right? Do the right things, believe the right things, and you'll make it, right?"[5]

Maybe that worked once upon a time. But many people are now finding they need to rethink and recast their own economic dreams. Les Falen, now in his late forties, is employed, but not at a job that pays well or has much of a career future. He described the American Dream he has had to revise: "To me the American Dream was always an upward spiral. You start out modest. As you move up, you make a step upward in lifestyle. That view began to change for me when we came back to California, where we had to pay more for the same things we had before. Then the American Dream became a matter of maintaining rather than moving ahead. But my experience has made me a lot more grateful for what we do have—we are healthy, we can take vacations, we do have enough to enjoy life. But as far as thinking next year will be a bigger vacation, that's gone out the window."

Another aspect Les has had to rethink is retirement. Like most people, Les looks at his father and compares his situation to his parents'. Instead of being better off than his parents, Les' future looks quite a bit dimmer. "My father for twenty years of retirement had no financial worries at all. My mom is now receiving more money in retirement than we're earning from our work. We grew up thinking that at age sixty-five, we should be able to quit working and keep the same lifestyle. Now, retirement seems like a fantasy. I can't see when I will be able to quit work. Now we are just making it through month by month."

Les' wife, Alice, has a different definition of the American Dream: "For me the American Dream is security—not having to struggle all the time."

However you perceive the American Dream, you probably were influenced by how you were raised. Beth Haines has found it hard to adjust to a more frugal lifestyle: "My father was never out of work, and the money was always there. My family doesn't approve of us." When her husband, Pete, lost his job and found one that was not as good as his previous one, he joined the ranks of the underemployed. Beth cared for other people's children in their home, but making ends meet was always in question. To cut back, they turned down recreational opportunities with others, so their social life has suffered. They took only a one-week vacation and a few long weekends, camping. ("I hate camping!" Beth said.) They used to go out to dinner together every couple of weeks; they cut that out. They have never bought new furniture. They buy few new clothes, and now the only cars they drive are used cars. ("I hate used cars and camping!" Beth said.) One of the worst things about the struggle is not knowing if leaner or fatter times lie ahead. They found it hard never to know when they could splurge without feeling guilty, never to know when or if they will ever achieve their dreams of "being further along" in life.

Losing the American Dream is especially bitter for those who once had it. One sixtyish executive explained: "Older execs like me were brought up during the Depression. Bankruptcy or failure to meet one's obligations was presented to us as an absolute disgrace. Being out of work for a long time can negate all your background and destroy the actual core of our belief in ourselves. It may ruin our ethical and moral fiber. I felt as if I have a runaway reactor inside me involved in a self-destructive chain reaction."[6]

But another husband and wife who have lost what they once thought was the American Dream, believe they are now better off. For a short time Tom and Norma Lorner lived the American Dream. They both worked, owned their own home, drove nice cars—but Tom and Norma saw each other for only an hour and a half each day. When Norma gave birth to their third child, they moved to a community with a lower cost of living and gave up their pursuit of prosperity. "We saw our friends build up their dreams, and often get divorced," Tom explained. "We decided we would pay our dues to be a family. We enjoy our kids." Though Norma could go back to work, she feels strongly that she doesn't want to "miss her kids" by putting them into full-time daycare.

Revising financial expectations and adjusting to downward mobility is never easy. But those who have done it, whether by choice or necessity, have found that not only is it possible but also there are unexpected rewards in doing so.

Review Your Finances

Many of us don't think about the fact that we might be only a paycheck or two away from losing our home or car. As long as the money keeps rolling in, we're lulled into a false sense of security. We don't always pay much attention to where the money goes. Once the paychecks stop, however, we're forced to pay attention. Too often we respond with panic. But this is no time for panic. It's time to think clearly and soberly about how to handle your money and what your values are. The sooner you deal with this harsh reality, the better off you'll be in bolstering your self-esteem, calming your spouse's fears, and developing confidence and clear thinking as you look for a new job or career.

Because money means so much—security, hope for the future, status—taking a clear look at the financial facts means getting past the symbolism. In order to do this, first talk with your spouse about your biggest financial fears. Karen Henderson was terrified of losing the house, the dream house she had decorated and landscaped herself. It wasn't until Greg sat down with her and went over all the figures about how much savings they had and what his plans were that her fears subsided.

LESSONS LEARNED

Without a doubt the financial aspects of a career trauma are some of the most painful and troubling. Paradoxically, people who have weathered the crisis report that the economic lessons they learned were some of the most valuable.

I remember a friend telling me, "It's one of my worst fears that my husband would lose his job. I don't know how we would survive." Well, those who have survived learn that they can face hard times and survive, even without a regular paycheck.

Many couples reported that their children learned valuable lessons in thrift, responsibility, and resourcefulness. Kids found ways to earn money or get what they needed despite the lack of money. Roberta Schaefer believes their cash flow crunch has been a good learning and character-building process for her five children. "We talk about recycling and reusing. For instance, if one of the boys wants a new bicycle, we see what we can find at a garage sale. We'll pitch in together and clean up the bike we buy. We'll talk about what would have happened to that bike if we hadn't bought it." She added, "I don't think it would be any different if we had money"; she and her husband would still want to instill these values in their children. They also work hard to counteract the materialism hawked by the media: "We have a lot of discussions about television commercials and what they are saying and how they are trying to make us buy their product," she said.

Les and Alice Falen also agreed that the skills of budgeting, deferring pleasure, having to plan ahead, and making choices are skills that will serve their children well. College freshman Laurie Brenner acknowledged that her father's repeated unemployment taught her to focus less on material things and to value people and life itself a lot more.

And almost everyone mentioned that the financial strains had a deeply spiritual side as well. They were forced to depend on God in new ways. Their faith in whether or not God would provide for them was tested. When their own resources and ability to depend on those resources gave way, the true nature of their faith was exposed. For many of the men, women, and children, the spiritual crisis was by far the deepest.

• 9 •

God, Where Are You?

Michael Catlin was no stranger to career trauma. The first time he was unemployed, it was because he left a job he felt compromised his integrity. He went back to school and finished a master's degree in finance. Ticket to a good job, right? That's what he thought it would be. But it took him nine months to find a banking job, and even then it wasn't as challenging as he would have liked. Then he was laid off a few months later, and it took him three months to find another job, as a management trainee at a bank. After a few months there, the bank merged with another, and Michael was laid off. That job drought lasted two and a half years. During that time he worked odd jobs, including one part-time consulting job that lasted a year and a half. During this whole period, Michael felt he continually took jobs to earn money; none was what he considered a career opportunity.

Michael struggled to make sense of his plight. "I felt I should be as successful as other people are," he said. "I had the credentials. I was doing what God has asked me to do. I wasn't sinning. So why am I not able to find work in my field?"

Like all of us, Michael carried a "mental map" of the way the world should work. According to Michael's map, if you get the education and do the right things, you should be able to find your place in the world. Michael was intelligent, personable, and industrious. He did all the things he was supposed to do to get a job—developed a network, sent out résumés, followed up every job lead. Yet reality wasn't cooperating; he was not finding the satisfying jobs that were supposed to be out there. Either something was wrong with him, or something was wrong with the way things were supposed to be. Michael fluctuated between blaming himself and blaming "The System." He prayed for a job, of course, but wasn't totally sure where God fit in. He supposed this was some kind of test, to improve his character somehow. He didn't see how: the emotional roller coaster made him difficult to live with, and he had withdrawn from friends and people from church because they had let him down. Knowing he wasn't handling the situation well only made him feel worse.

Michael's crisis was more than emotional, more than financial, more than social. At its core, it was a spiritual crisis. It tore large holes in his map of how reality works, and he was forced to undertake the painful task of revising that map.

I believe that career trauma is a spiritual crisis for all of us, whether we hold to a formal religion or not. All of us construct some mental map of reality. All of us strive to make sense of our experience. We think we understand how the world works until one day something happens to throw into question those beliefs, and we are forced to revise our maps. The stronger our convictions, the more painful it is to give up or change those convictions once they are proved false in some way. That is why it may be more difficult for someone who has strong views about God and spiritual things to go through job trauma than for someone whose beliefs are more vague.

For instance, I had always believed that God gives each

one of us gifts, that he wants us to use our gifts for good in the world, and that if we seek him, he will provide us opportunities to use our gifts in fulfilling work. I followed this map faithfully, and it worked for me: I held on to my dreams and always found fulfilling jobs.

Then I met and married Gene. He did not have fulfilling work when I married him; I figured it was just a matter of a little time before he got on track with what he should be doing with his life. I nudged—no, to be honest, I pushed—him toward the direction I thought he should go. Secretly, I felt he was sinning by not being willing to follow the tried and true methods of Richard Bolles and other experts who know how to help people find a job they can love. Isn't it a sin to waste one's talents? Gene is intelligent, he has a graduate degree, he has many talents—why couldn't he just settle on something and go for it? Why was God not supplying the opportunities for Gene as he always had for me?

Searching for answers to these questions forced me to look at Gene, God, reality, and myself in new ways. It stretched my faith to its limits. Eventually I learned that stretching led to a larger faith, a larger view of God, and perhaps a larger, more tolerant view of my husband and myself.

In the end, the questions may be more important than the answers.

WHERE ARE YOU, GOD?

Consciously or subconsciously, we ask God lots of questions: Why is this happening to me? What are you trying to teach me? What am I doing wrong? Are you punishing me? Why can't I find work to match the gifts I have? But beneath all these questions is the real question: God, where are you? How could you let this happen to me if you really love me?

We feel God has abandoned us. Sometimes we feel God

has abandoned us because we feel his people have abandoned us. Jim Stacks became a Christian at age thirty, got involved in the Episcopal church, and eventually received a strong call to the ministry. He went to seminary and became a priest. He worked in an urban church for several years, then became rector of a small congregation that grew in both numbers and spiritual depth. Sensing it was time for a change, he accepted the request from his diocese to serve as an interim specialist at a church seeking a permanent pastor. Though all signs pointed toward success, he was told he was not going to get another interim position and would be out of work indefinitely.

Unemployment shattered many illusions Jim didn't even know he had, such as the illusion that the church will take care of its clergy. "I knew I had done a good job, but to be suddenly out on the street without benefits, without assurance of medical benefits at a time when my wife was very sick—there was no security. I had no sense that my bishops had a clue what it was like for me. It left me feeling very alone," he said.

Brett Parrish worked for a religious organization. Soon it became clear that he had a major personality conflict with his boss. Brett tried everything he could to change to fit his boss' needs, but he found himself out of a job anyway. What stung him the most was that none of the board members, whom Brett had felt were friends, ever called him after he left the job. It was as if those relationships had never been formed.

The rebuke not to air their laundry in their Sunday school class cut Michael and Martha Catlin so deeply because they felt abandoned by God's people in their pain. This was especially devastating to the Catlins because at the time, they desperately needed other people's support. They felt unable to pray for themselves or each other.

Other people also described similar times of spiritual dryness. They were so emotionally spent by the effort to cope with all the aspects of their crisis that they could not feel God's presence at all. When other Christians don't respond with support and kindness, people undergoing the crisis feel abandoned.

If you feel God has abandoned you, start by acknowledging that fact. But remember: your feelings are not reliable indications of what the facts are. You may feel God has abandoned you, but he certainly hasn't. What is happening is that your old religion—whatever was the real source of your security in this life—is crumbling. Now is the ideal time to rebuild, to forge a personal faith that is big enough to sustain you through this crisis. Here are suggestions to guide you through this grieving and rebuilding process.

ANGER WITH GOD

Not only do people feel abandoned by God, but they also feel angry with him. Mitch Grisweiler remembered, "Early in my unemployment I was so focused on the problem that God and I were not on speaking terms. I didn't want to talk to him or listen to anything he had to say. It was a vicious cycle—it led to more frustration and a low view of my own spirituality."

Mitch suppressed his emotions for a while, ignoring his anger until it boiled over in shouting matches with God. "I would shout, 'What is going on? You've given me abilities and desires, then you take away the opportunities. What is going on? What is it about me that needs this? It must be something terrible!'"

Roberta Schaefer admitted to being very angry with God too. "Why do I have to go through this?" she would cry, beating her pillow.

Our anger and questions are part of the grief process. We grieve the death of our old way of seeing reality, and we seek to form a new map with clearer meaning.

RECONFIGURE THE MAP

Vic Glavach had been searching for a job for fifteen months when he hit one of his lowest points. He had appointments lined up in several states, starting in Miami and working his way back north. One situation seemed especially hopeful: out of more than 160 applicants, the company had narrowed the list to six. Vic was on that list.

He thought the interview went well. But by the time he reached home after his next stops, a letter had already arrived. A rejection letter. "Sorry, you're not the person we wanted for the job." Vic just sank into a chair, utterly defeated.

"In the days that followed," Vic said, "I took a long look at my goals and at my relationship with God. It isn't that I lost my faith, but I reevaluated the 'you scratch my back and I'll scratch yours' attitude we tend to get into with God when we experience difficult times."

Late one night he walked around the neighborhood alone, virtually shaking his fist at God and asking out loud, "Why? Where are you? What's wrong with me?" Yet even as he blurted out the words in the darkness, he knew he and his family were surviving only because God was caring for them.[1]

This conflict of emotions and knowledge repeatedly surfaced in people's experience. What has to die is an inadequate view of God, mixed up with a faulty view of reality. As Bob Hicks points out in his book *Uneasy Manhood*, many people have an underlying philosophy he calls meritocracy: if you do your best, you will get ahead; the good wins over the bad in the end. An employment crisis shoots a hole in that philosophy. You may have done your job, but you didn't get ahead. Furthermore, some of your colleagues who kept their jobs may not have been as honest or as hardworking as you have been. You have been a good person, you have followed the rules, so why is this happening to you? A career crisis has a way of unmasking deep-rooted assumptions about the way life works, and these assumptions can, if we let them, pull us closer to a more biblical philosophy of life.

Gene had to revise the view of life and manhood passed down to him from his father, who didn't like his job and struggled a lot with life because of it. Because Gene loved his dad and felt he had done a lot of things right as a parent, it was hard to admit his father had failed him in some crucial ways. But his dad had failed him. Where he should have given Gene direction, he gave him nothing. No direction about vocation. No talk about work or the future. Gene had to come to terms with that lack and with the ways he had tried to make up for it. He had no trouble seeing that "The System" was faulty—his father had taught him that. But the way he subsequently tried to minimize the place of vocation wasn't working for Gene either. Like many men, he basically had to throw out the faulty map he had been handed down and start from ground zero in constructing an accurate and biblical view of work and his own gifts. It was a painful and often lonely road. But he said, "My view of reality really did have to change in order for me to come to a fuller appreciation of who I am and what I have to offer."

Gene's crisis precipitated one of my own, not uncommon with a job crisis. I also had to revise my views about vocation to include Gene's reality. I still believe that it's a worthy goal to find work that uses one's gifts. But Gene's experience has shown me that this world is broken, people are broken, "The System" is broken. Not everything is going to run the way it should—not even when we pray and trust God and do everything right. Like Vic, I have had to revise my view of God and my relationship to him. I had to face the fact that what I really wanted was for God to always make everything better. I wanted to escape pain. But God seems to have a different agenda. Accepting his agenda for this hard time was part of my spiritual challenge, just as accepting his father's failures was part of Gene's.

Michael Catlin also found his faith undergoing a metamorphosis. "My faith had been to some degree in 'The System': if you do everything you're supposed to do, you will get the result," he admitted. "But now my faith is deeper; that's one of the biggest changes. I still think God is in control of who gets the job and who doesn't, and we often don't understand his purposes. Sometimes you can do everything all right and it still doesn't turn out okay—but that doesn't mean God isn't in control. We may pray fervently for a job and not get it. I don't have all the answers, and I can't get them. I have to trust and obey even if I don't see the results."

This painful period also showed Michael some uncomfortable things about himself. He spoke of uncovering an attitude that God owed him something. He said, "It struck me recently, was I worshiping God or the gifts he gives? The real centrality of our faith is God himself and not the things he gives us, like jobs. During rough circumstances God gives us himself. He lets us undergo these times for his own good purposes, which we may not even understand if he told us."

I agree with Michael that we may not always understand God's purposes. But I have found that if we ask, God often does give us some sense of a larger purpose. And this can be an important step to getting through the crisis not only with our faith intact but also with a deeper sense of his love and care for us.

The first step is realizing that something has to die—our old philosophy of life and our inadequate view of God. We have to grieve that death. And then we can move on to accept the new life that can spring up in its place.

Don't Dodge the Deeper Questions

Often the losses trigger other, deeper issues that must be dealt with before we can move on with ourselves, God, and each other. For Jim Stacks, losing his job stirred something very painful, relating to his idea of home. When the church let him go, he found himself strongly resisting the idea of relocating. He finally sorted it all out: "Now that I've lost my home in the church, I can't give up my other home. I felt like an emotionally and spiritually homeless person." He shared these insights with his spiritual director, with whom he met regularly before and during his career crisis. The director asked him if he could find his home in God. "That question was a gift of grace," Jim said reflectively. "That has been the spiritual foundation of this journey for me: rediscovering my home in God."

Perhaps each of us wrestles with a unique demon in the midst of our crisis. As I mentioned, for Gene it was admitting his father had failed him in certain ways. Until he saw the connection between his father and his employment struggles, though, his demon was the sense of failure and inadequacy: "Other people were moving on and I wasn't," he said. "I assumed other people got from their father the same things I did, so my problem must have been that something was wrong with me." Realizing that his father had not given him any guidance in a crucial area was a breakthrough, but the breakthrough brought still more pain: it produced an explanation, but also "a crack in the image" Gene had of his dad. Understanding and accepting his past and moving on to a sense of his unique gifts required hard work and an honesty that could only be grounded in the faith that God was in control and did have a plan for his life. From my perspective, I believe Gene's faith is stronger, he is stronger, and his relationships are more honest as a result of his experience. It was a case of God bringing good things out of painful times.

Don't shove away the uncomfortable and painful questions that whisper to you in your dark moments. Rather, embrace them. Open your heart. Listen to what the question is asking. But don't do it alone! Ask God to be with you. Talk to a friend, pastor or spiritual director, or therapist—someone who understands the process of spiritual growth, someone who can allow you to doubt and question. Gene said he probably could not have worked through his issues without his faith and the support of a few wise counselors.

DISCOVER A LARGER VIEW OF GOD

I like what Michael Catlin said: "During the rough times God gives us himself." He doesn't necessarily give us a wonderful job or more money or an end to our pain. He gives us himself.

In order to accept this gift, we have to be willing to allow him to change our view of who he is. Many people like to quote a familiar Bible verse, Revelation 3:20: "Here I am! I stand at the door and knock. If anyone hears my voice and opens the door, I will come in and eat with him, and he with me." This is a wonderful picture of Jesus entering our lives and communing with us. But notice the preceding verse: "Those whom I love I rebuke and discipline. So be earnest, and repent." Jesus seems to be saying that he wants to come into our lives, but before we can hear his knock, we may have to accept his rebuke and discipline, and repent.

Repent of what? Most often, I think, we need to repent of the faulty views we have of God and open the door to the true God as he reveals himself. I am finding that it involves a continual process of shedding my old false views of who God is and seeing him for who he truly is. So many of the false views are bound up with my personal experiences and my parents. I believe that parents leave a profound spiritual imprint on their children; the parents hand the children the spiritual glasses through which they will interpret the world. Growing up spiritually means removing the glasses and retraining our vision to see the world the way God says it truly is.

I know of no better way of discarding a faulty view of

God and gaining a true vision than studying and meditating on God's revelation, the Bible. Catechisms like the Heidelberg or the Westminster Confession of Faith are also good for gaining a systematic, biblical view of how God has revealed himself. Brett Parrish pulled out his Heidelberg Catechism and read question after question, telling how these words have helped him reform his perspective. Quoting from Question 27, he read, "'He still upholds everything . . . all things come to us not by chance but by his fatherly hand. . . .' In evangelical circles," Brett continued thoughtfully, "we haven't really understood the providence of God, that he works actively in the world even in the midst of suffering. We've been conditioned to an escapist mentality, but that's not biblical faith. We need to accept God's working in the world and not expect everything's going to be rosy.

"At one time I was asking God to rescue me from my situation. But now I'm asking him to help me respond with faith, hope, and love, and not expect a job next week." Brett was wrestling with doctrines that are not just dusty axioms but matters that will make or break how he survives a prolonged job crisis.

If an employment crisis has set off a spiritual crisis for you, re-examine your idea of God. What is it you doubt the most? His love? That was Pam Grisweiler's stumbling block for a time. *If you really love me, God,* she thought, *you won't let this job crisis continue.* But one day the truth of Romans 8:32 hit her: "He who did not spare his own Son, but gave him up for us all—how will he not also, along with him, graciously give us all things?" Her doubt gave way under the weight of this firm promise.

Perhaps you struggle to understand why God allowed this to happen to you. Another of the faulty views I had to revise was the secret belief that somehow, God's people should be spared hard times. I had to remind myself that hard times come to believer and unbeliever alike: "Dear friends, do not be surprised at the painful trial you are suffering, as though something strange were happening to you," Scripture says (1 Peter 4:12).

I also had to pin down exactly what I believed about God's sovereignty—the fact that he controls everything—and human free will. God does not cause the hard times; fallen, sinful human beings and fallen, sinful human institutions do that. But God allows them to happen for a larger purpose, and he intends to bring something good out of the pain. And, in the midst of the pain, he gives us himself—"Thine own dear presence, to cheer and to guide," as the hymn "Great Is Thy Faithfulness" proclaims.

His presence, I am discovering, can make all the difference. With his presence comes change—if not in our circumstances, then certainly in our perspective. With his presence comes hope, strength, and peace. Roberta Schaefer said that she and Kyle are probably financially worse off now than they've ever been, but she's never been more contented. Her contentment comes from a sense of God's presence, a security that is built on specific evidence of God's daily care for them.

Finally, with God's presence as sustainer, strengthener, and deliverer, comes joy. Dr. David Jeremiah, expounding the Book of Romans, pointed out that a Christian can be in heaviness and still be "greatly rejoicing." Someone has said that a Christian is someone who has superficial sadness and central gladness. I have found this to be true, and so have many of the people I interviewed. On the surface, we encounter so many trials and all the emotions that come from dealing with job loss, living on a reduced income, seeing many of our dreams and hopes for this life fade away, perhaps never to be revived. Yet on a deeper level, we are finding a richer purpose. And with that sense of meaning, we feel a strange joy. Victor Frankl is often quoted as saying, "He who has a *why* to live can bear with almost any *how*." If you don't have a sense of why you are going through this crisis, seeking that perspective is your next step.

Seek the Larger Perspective

Perspective is everything.

Nora and Bud Bower thought Bud's employment crisis was over when, after six months, he finally found another job that he liked. Nora remembers the day she went out to buy a camcorder so they could videotape their teenage son's wrestling matches. After researching which stores had the best prices, she drove thirty miles to the store that had a sale. As soon as she approached the electronics section, a store clerk came up and said to her, "Are you Nora Bower?" Startled, she replied, "Yes." How on earth would a store clerk know her name?

"Your husband called and said to call home as soon as you get here," the clerk said. "You can use the phone in the office there."

Her heart in her throat, Nora dialed home. In the eternity it took for Bud to answer the phone, she pictured a dozen disasters: Bud got in an accident; one of the kids was maimed or bleeding in the middle of the road, or . . . something worse. When Bud finally answered, she could barely choke out, "What happened?"

Bud said, "I just lost my job. Don't buy the camcorder; we can't afford it now." Nora felt like laughing. Is that all it was? Compared to the disasters she envisioned, this was almost nothing. They had been down this road before, and they had survived.

Nora saw that incident as a gift, frightening though it was. All the way home, instead of feeling terrible that Bud lost his job, all she felt was grateful—grateful that the call was not for something worse. When she got home, Bud was lying on the sofa in the dark, wrapped up in a blanket. He was very depressed about losing his job again. But when Nora shared the thoughts that had raced through her mind when the clerk approached her and how grateful she was that something worse hadn't happened, Bud felt a little better. Yes, he agreed, they had been down this road, and they had survived. He would get another job, and in the meantime they would certainly not starve. The following period of unemployment, which lasted only three months, was much easier to weather because they reminded themselves that this was not the worst thing that could happen to them.

For four years, Bob Marone struggled to make peace with a job he did not like. He didn't have a lot to choose from in the rural area where he lived, but he kept looking for something more fulfilling. Relocation was a possibility, but his wife, Kerry, refused to move unless he had a secure job to move to.

Bob moved through several stages of employment crisis, from feeling hopeful to finally giving up. He sank into a depression, dissatisfied with his house, his station in life, his community. He withdrew from friends and family because he felt inferior for not having a better job.

It became a spiritual issue, especially for Kerry, who had a strong faith. She prayed and clung to her faith and did her best to support Bob. And slowly, somehow, Bob changed. He deepened his relationship to God, renewed his commitment to his church, and found new solace in prayer. Nothing else changed—he still disliked his job, they still lived in the same cramped house, they still didn't have much money. But Bob's perspective shifted dramatically as a result of his spiritual reawakening. He realized he was fortunate even to have a job; so many people in the recession-wracked New England area didn't have jobs. He began to focus more on what he did have: a wife who loves him, two wonderful children, a house in a safe neighborhood where his children could put down roots, a church community. The Bob I interviewed four years ago—depressed and dissatisfied with his job, his life, himself—was a very different Bob from the man whose voice now dripped peace and acceptance of himself and his lot. And Kerry confirmed that the changes seemed permanent.

In the quest for a larger perspective, the Bible is again invaluable. In reading the Bible, we realize that our story is just a subplot in a much grander story. Once we see this, we are in a position to receive God's wisdom. We can begin to trust that he has a larger purpose to what we are enduring.

In looking to the Bible, I think of Job, the classic case of someone who suffered deeply. And in the end, what did God do? Did he explain to Job what readers know from the first chapter? No. What God did was reveal himself and his power; he dragged Job's focus from his problems to God and his greatness. The best way to get wisdom from God, Larry Crabb says, is to look first at God and the story of what he is doing and then to see ourselves and our problems in the context of this larger story. This will bring us hope.

Karen Volpert, who directs the Career Crossroads ministry to the unemployed in Wayne, Pennsylvania, conducts an annual seminar in which the participants study the career paths of men God used mightily in biblical history. Moses lived in relative obscurity for forty years—count 'em, forty years—before God gave him his great assignment to lead God's chosen people out of slavery. Joseph was on a great career path until he suddenly lost everything and ended up in a prison for years. God eventually delivered him and again brought him to a position of power and authority. The apostle Paul found that the more he served God, the more he encountered opposition and trials. Any one of these people may have felt God had forgotten them during these periods of obscurity and seeming unproductivity, but God was using that time for his purposes.

Seeking a larger perspective also involves actively focusing on the positive things that develop during a job crisis. Roberta Schaefer is living a life much different from the one she expected. She and Kyle and their five children are just scraping by financially as Kyle works some odd jobs and follows his dream of writing film scripts. Their situation has forced her to reconsider her views of God, for one thing. "I grew up thinking God would take care of me, but in the way I thought he would. I had to re-examine the boxes I put God in." Looking over the past ten years, she can see that God has brought them through. He has provided, but not in the ways she had expected.

Pride was the first thing to go. "I can't yet ask for help, but I'm not as embarrassed to let people know our situation and accept help when it's offered." She wishes she could be on the giving end more frequently, but she speculated, "Maybe God was using me to help other people learn to give."

Roberta's situation also forced her to take another look at the basis on which she sets a person's value. Like many of us, she grew up with conditional love; you were good if you did things right. "You learn to value yourself for what you do rather than what you are. I'm learning to love myself for being who I am. If I get up and I don't do the laundry that day, am I a failure? No, because I am who God created me to be."

This lesson has also transferred to how she sees her husband. The question, "What does your husband do?" doesn't bother Roberta as much as it used to. She is also learning to value him for who he is, not for what he does.

Take time to ask God what he wants you to be doing with yourself besides looking for a job. He may have some other valuable purpose in mind.

Looking back, the Catlins have a sense of God's timing in each of Michael's periods of unemployment. The first time, when he left his job voluntarily, Martha became very sick and was hospitalized. The doctors didn't know what was wrong, and they weren't sure she would even live. Martha remembers how Michael was constantly at her side, encouraging her, assuring her he loved her no matter what happened. She doesn't know how she would have gotten through that time if he had not been so available. And, during the last long period of unemployment, Michael spent the first eight months settling "a mess of an estate" that Martha's father left when he died, just four months before Michael lost his job. "If Michael had not been available to do that work, it would have been absolutely horrible," Martha believes. "God provided Michael with an opportunity to serve me and to minister to me in a way that he could not have done if he had been working full time at a paying job."

Martha and Michael are able to look back and see God's faithfulness in the midst of hard times, and that has become an anchor for them in the future. In what painful circumstances have you seen God's presence and purposes? What biblical truth have you learned through these circumstances? How have these truths anchored you?

One woman whose husband faced job uncertainty told of losing her home through a fire. As she struggled to deal with the loss, she took a walk in the woods and sat on a rock by a stream. Looking down, she noticed little plants—periwinkles, she thought they were—growing out of the water. How on earth could they survive being buffeted from the waterfall above? she wondered. And then, it was as if a still voice said, "They survive because they cling to the rock." And that is how she too would survive, she realized: by clinging to the Rock that is God. Peace flooded her soul as she realized that God didn't expect her to do anything more than cling to him, trusting that he is in control.

Trust that your pain has purpose, that God is in control, that he is bringing good out of bad. Ask him to open your eyes to his hand in your life, both past and present. And then, take the next step: thank him for who he is and what he has given you.

Practice Gratitude

Recently I came across the following Scripture passage: "Sacrifice thank offerings to God, fulfill your vows to the Most High, and call upon me in the day of trouble; I will deliver you, and you will honor me. . . . He who sacrifices thank offerings honors me, and he prepares the way so that I may show him the salvation of God" (Ps. 50:14–15, 23). According to these verses, giving thanks somehow prepares the way for us to experience God's help and deliverance.

Thankfulness has a wonderful way of turning our focus to the positive. Rather than focusing on what we didn't have—a well-paying job for Gene—I began to thank God for what he had provided: cars that continued to run despite an average mileage of 100,000 each; appliances that have not had to be replaced; relatively good health. Again, I gained perspective. And my mood changed, from gloom to hope.

Gratitude is also one of the best ways to build our faith. As I thank God for the ways he has provided, I also affirm that he will continue to provide in the future. And so my faith is strengthened. Even if I feel so bad that I can't think of anything to thank God for, I can thank him that he is with me, whether or not I feel he is there. As I affirm God's promises and thank him for whatever I can, I develop an attitude of expectation that God will continue to act on my behalf. I open my eyes to his work in my life. And with that, I am able to do what I need to do: move on through the crisis, receive grace from God and from others, and learn how to give grace to my spouse, other people, and myself.

Part II

Coping Strategies for Individuals, Families, Churches, and Communities

· 10 ·

Help Yourself Move On

I t's like being thrown on an Outward Bound trip you didn't choose to take—an odyssey into the job-hunting wilderness," wrote one job seeker about the rigors of the job search.[1] Whether you're unemployed, underemployed, or unhappily employed, looking for a satisfying job is a stressful activity.

That's why this book has emphasized the importance of grieving the losses and dealing with the emotional, interpersonal, and spiritual issues first. Once you have done this, you'll have the energy you need to embark on your job search.

That doesn't mean you do nothing until all your grief is past. It's more a matter of emphasis, of focus: what should be central at any given time, and what is more peripheral? At first the grieving process is central, even while you pull together a résumé and begin to develop your network. Once you work through the issues, you will find energy building and will naturally be able to put more effort into the mechanics of the job search.

Adopt a Healthy Perspective

Doing something helps us feel we are making progress. Action counterbalances the helplessness that can lead so easily to depression and anxiety. Working through your losses is one way of taking action because it does move you through grief to the other side. The next steps are to conduct a thorough inventory of yourself and to develop a job-search strategy. Taking action in these ways is the best way to improve your attitude and generate hope.

Adopt this perspective: your current job is to look for a satisfying job. Treat it as seriously as you did your job. If you're unemployed, you can give this full-time attention. If you're working part time, you can make time to conduct a job search. If you're underemployed but working full time, this process may be toughest for you. But don't let that deter you. Take each step, realizing that it will take you longer. With each step you will gain some momentum and hope.

Remember to pursue at least one other interest or commitment totally outside the job search. This reaffirms that you are more than a job, more than a paycheck-generator. You are a human being, with numerous skills, interests, and abilities that will help other people. Gary Brighton didn't feel devastated by his job loss, largely because he had been active as an elder in his church, a commitment that continued after he became unemployed and that gave him a sense of continuity and purpose. Keeping active in something you enjoy may pave the way to important job leads. And pursuing something for the pure joy of it will lessen the stress and affirm your value as a person.

Examine your expectations and be realistic. It will take a while to find a job that fits you. The old formula was to expect to spend a month in the job search for every $10,000 in salary you expect to earn; some outplacement experts believe that time period needs to be doubled. If your job target is an executive position with a salary of $100,000, it may take ten to twenty months to find that job. You will need to develop not only a strategy for finding a job but also a strategy for surviving emotionally, spiritually, socially, and financially during your unemployment.

You also need to take charge of your own future and learn something about our rapidly changing world. In the workplace of the 1990s and beyond, experts believe that more people will be structurally unemployed—without a job because technology has made their jobs obsolete. In the past, street sweepers, buggy-whip makers, and shoemakers faced this kind of structural unemployment. Today's rapidly advancing technology has also made aerospace scientists and engineers, auto workers, tire makers, steel workers, and farm laborers structurally unemployed. Their challenge is to take their skills and apply them to new industries or to train for another career. This demands an attitude of continual learning, continual refining of skills, an openness to new ideas and new ways of doing things.

Some career counselors advise taking a whole new attitude toward your career. In "the old days" (meaning six or seven years ago!), many people could count on working for the same company throughout most of their career and retire with a good pension. Those days are gone, and we may as well face it. Rather than seeing your career as one set thing (I am an auto maker or pilot or computer programmer or . . .), begin to think of yourself as "a person who makes things or is in charge of people or analyzes data or . . ." Don't try to marry a job "till death do you part." In the world of careers, serial monogamy is the way to go. Your career as a whole is a series of projects, undertaken with various partners (otherwise known as employers), at various times. Rather than see yourself as an employee in search of an employer, see yourself as a consultant in search of a company that needs your particular skills to solve its particular problems at a particular time. At times, for whatever reason, your skills and the company's needs don't match. Then it will be time to move on, voluntarily or involuntarily. This attitude tends to depersonalize the job hunt and help you be more objective.

Expect rejections. Remind yourself, daily if you have to, that a job hunt is largely a numbers game. Salespeople know that they need so many dozen contacts before anyone even shows interest, and that out of those who show some interest, only a few will close the sale. You are now a salesperson selling a product: your time, talents, and energy. Somewhere out there are companies and people who want what you have to offer, but it will take time and lots of contacts to uncover those. You may also need to convince a company that your skills match its needs. Don't take the inevitable rejections personally. Instead, tell yourself, "Oh well, that didn't work out. On to the next possibility!"

Of course, rejection will sometimes necessitate going back and doing some grieving, especially if you had your expectations up because you were one of the top candidates for a job you really wanted. My husband and Vic Glavach both said they felt most defeated when they had been closest to being chosen. It's almost impossible not to let your hopes rise. In fact, it's important to maintain a sense of positive expectation rather than to despair and give up.

Four Stages of Unemployment

As you look for work, you probably will go through four predictable stages.[2] These stages are different from the stages of handling loss and change (outlined in chapter 2). By understanding these stages, you can identify where you are and what you might need most at this time.

Stage 1: "I'm not unemployed—just in between jobs." (1–2 months) The first few months of unemployment may be a fairly relaxed time. You may feel more like you're "between jobs" rather than unemployed. You may feel fairly optimistic and confident. Rather than jump into the job search right away, you may take some time to relax, do projects around the house, take more time to be with family, or pursue a hobby.

This time for many people is a time to rebalance life and "catch up" on projects they always wanted to do. Greg Henderson reported that he enjoyed this period and spent lots of time with his children.

Stage 2: "I'm giving it my best shot." (2–6 months) In this stage you make an all-out effort to find a job. You update your résumé, respond to ads, make calls. You feel encouraged by conversations with those in your network. Family and friends are usually supportive and somewhat involved. While some anxiety may be building, you still feel considerable optimism, especially at the beginning. The longer this stage continues, the lower and shorter the "highs" and the deeper and longer the "lows" of the emotional roller coaster.

Stage 3: "Things may never change." (4–6 months and on) This third stage is a time of self-doubt and near desperation as you bounce between despair and frantic attempts to find work. You may enter this stage if you face a jobless period that is longer than you've experienced before or if you are unemployed for the second time within a short period. You begin to wonder if you ever will get a job, at least one you want. You may wonder if you have been going about the search the right way or if you should make some sort of career change. The spiritual issues we examined come up in this stage.

With the intense mood swings, the search for work is much more sporadic, with occasional bursts of energy and activity alternating with longer periods of inactivity. You may become very critical, blaming, and angry with yourself. You may alternate between lashing out and sinking into depression.

Family relationships often become strained at this point. The anger and frustration often get "dumped" on the family, and family members will sometimes dump their frustration in other places, like school or groups. Friends seem less helpful, less interested in being involved, and the loneliness grows.

Stage 3 will continue for several months—perhaps as long as a year and a half or two years—before Stage 4 takes over.

Stage 4: "I give up." In the fourth stage, you quit the job search. This period is marked by cynicism and malaise. It is a self-protective stage, when you are not willing to face the pain or risk further rejection in the prolonged search. Energy level sinks, and attempts to find work are infrequent. You may find yourself telling other people that you are retired.

When new job opportunities develop, you may be quite skeptical and may undermine a good job possibility in order not to risk another blow to your self-esteem. You feel pessimistic, powerless, angry, hostile, depressed, and, in extreme cases, even suicidal.

As time goes on, however, your emotions stabilize. Family relationships also stabilize. Often roles are shifted or shared more equally in the marriage. The family comes to accept the unemployment as a new reality—the new state of "normal." Friendships are more stable, but they are restricted to a few people. For some unemployed people, Stage 4 becomes permanent.

If you're in Stage 3 or 4, and find yourself unable to muster the energy to focus your efforts on developing a plan of action, you may need professional help. Ask for referrals from a pastor or social worker or professionals who will charge on a sliding scale or who will donate their services.

Do seek help if you're stuck, but seek it wisely. Realize that many therapists and counselors have not had training in the problems related to work life. They may not realize that many problems of unemployment result from the condition itself, and they may mistake the mechanical depression of unemployment for physiological depression. What you need is someone who can help you grieve your losses and move on to gainful employment. Now is not the time to psychoanalyze your past to death. If problems from the past are uncovered (which is likely), once you're employed, you will have the time (and the money and perhaps the insurance coverage) to deal with those issues more fully. Now your focus must be on finding a good job. Once you do that, some of your problems will automatically clear up. You'll then have the energy to deal with the problems that need further attention.

"It's always too soon to give up," Dr. V. Raymond Edman, former president of Wheaton College, was fond of saying. That is true for you. There is always hope. Job-placement counselors point to overwhelming statistics showing that people who keep working at it eventually do find a good job. The key is finding the strength and support to overcome the discouragement and stick to the task.

DEVELOP AN ACTION PLAN

A major part of that strength and support will come from developing an action plan. Plan weekly and daily goals as you work through the following steps. I suggest you write down on a simple chart your ultimate objective, the steps you need to take, the resources needed for each step (books, training, professional advice, people, etc.), your target date for completion, and what you will do to reward yourself or celebrate when you have completed each step. Don't omit this last step. You probably already know how long, tedious, and discouraging the job search is at times. Rewarding positive action will encourages you to continue and will help keep your energy level high.

Step 1: Establish Your Support Group

You need various kinds of support. Ideally, family and close friends want to be supportive and helpful, and if they are, by all means accept their offers. But if you're in the midst of a career crisis, you need a unique kind of support system outside those who are close to you. You need someone who understands exactly what you are going through and who can encourage you, support you, and hold you accountable for your job search. Such a support system can be an individual, such as a mentor or a person who is willing to help you keep on track as you look for work. Or the support can come from a group. Look for people or a group that will give you support, accountability, and objectivity. (Chapter 12 will look at the various kinds of support systems that are available through churches and communities.)

You may want to handpick your support group: someone who will agree to pray with you regularly; someone else who has been unemployed and who is willing to hold you accountable for doing the steps of a job search; someone who is employed in your field and who is willing to help you polish your professional and presentation skills.

If you're struggling with shame and isolation, you need a support group all the more. In fact, a group might be best for you, at least at first. One person called her job club "AA for the unemployed." That description was apt, because one of the main things it did for members was relieve the stigma of being unemployed because they saw so many other people in the same situation. Do whatever you have to do to force yourself to seek and attend such a group. Sharing with others who are experiencing exactly what you are will provide untold encouragement. If one support group doesn't suit you, find another one. Find a group in which you feel comfortable.

Step 2: Take Time to Evaluate

Dave Swanson, chief of staff for Richard Bolles' Parachute workshop, says that the big secret for finding satisfying work can be summed up in four words: "First, accuracy. Then, momentum." What he means by this is you first have to know yourself. What passion motivates you? What would you love to do even if no one paid you for it? What have you enjoyed doing in the past, and why? What do you dream of accomplishing with your life? What gets you excited? What seems to come easily to you? What has God blessed in your life in the past?

You can use a number of tools to help you discover your unique design—that constellation of skills, interests, and aptitudes that, if allowed expression, will bring you deep satisfaction. One of my favorite assessment tools is outlined in appendix A. If you're not sure where you want to go with your career or if you find yourself needing to adapt your skills to a new field because of limited opportunities in your former line of work, work through the exercises in appendix A before taking any of the next steps.

Too many people skip this step, thinking it will take too long. It may take a while, it's true, but generally it's more like an unfolding and a refocusing as you go along in your career. Because absolutely no job is secure in the present economy, we all need to have a Plan B and even a Plan C for our careers. Knowing your skills, dreams, interests, and strengths gives you the edge in seeing opportunities you might have overlooked.

Let's take Barry Crull, the unemployed airline pilot, as a case in point. Barry loved to fly, absolutely loved it. "It was like being in heaven," he said. "I would say to my co-pilot, 'I can't imagine any job more perfect.'" Obviously, Barry had a lot to grieve over when he lost his job. And because he loved his job so much, it was hard for him to imagine doing anything else.

Within a short period of time Barry found another job as a pilot. It was a definite step down in salary and prestige—he flew a turboprop rather than the jet he was used to—but that's not why he quit after only nineteen days. He quit because he felt he wasn't being treated right. Then in his desperation for a job, any job, Barry began selling used cars. He quickly realized that everything about that job was wrong: he received no training, the atmosphere was very cutthroat, and he found he wasn't comfortable in sales. He quit after two days.

Barry is learning the hard way that jumping into a job that's wrong for him is not a solution. In exploring with Barry just what he loved about flying, we uncovered some interesting things: he loved talking to the people. He loved maneuvering the aircraft. He relished being in the cockpit, especially at night when the moon and stars were out and everything was so peaceful and quiet.

Barry is taking time to evaluate his skills from a broad perspective and is coming up with more viable options: teaching other pilots or inspecting aircraft. He's quite willing to move or to get retrained to find other ways to use his strong technical and people skills in some field outside aviation.

An architect who was out of work learned the value of defining himself more broadly and being willing to "trade down" until things turn around in his field. He is pursuing several options: doing rehabilitation work, especially for firms that must conform with federal laws mandating easy access for disabled people; becoming a city planner, even a city manager; doing interior design; or becoming a consultant. He is also doing free work in his community to build his professional reputation.

You will find great freedom in defining yourself and your

career broadly. Hope ignites as you see that you are a multi-faceted person with a number of valuable skills. You overcome the feeling of being a victim of the economy as you educate yourself about options in various fields and come up with several possible directions. You become more open to exploring new fields, such as starting your own business or realizing your secret dreams. I believe you also allow God to open doors that you may not have noticed before.

When you have a strong sense of how you are uniquely gifted and what you are motivated to do—what writer Janis Long Harris calls "gifted passions"—you can communicate that to others.[3] "First, accuracy"—know yourself and your mission. "Then, momentum"—carry on your job search.

Step 3: Get Your Finances in Order

After working through the emotional issues, you need to take a hard look at your cash flow. That means starting a budget, if you haven't already done so. Only by knowing how much regularly goes out can you decide where you can cut back.

You can find good budgeting books from office-supply stores, create your own form with a ledger pad, or use a computer software program for home budgeting. Your budget should cover the categories as shown in the chart on the following page.

This budget sheet will help you begin to account for your monthly income and expenses. If you have not lived before on a budget, make several copies of this sheet and get your checkbook, bills, statements, and receipts for the past three months. Your goal is to arrive at two totals for each month: what you've earned and what you've spent. First, total up all your income for each of the three months. Then for each month, list what you have spent in each of these categories and arrive at a total for all of your monthly expenses.

SAMPLE BUDGET

Income

salary/wages _____
social security _____
pension _____
interest _____
dividends _____
unemployment
  compensation _____
other _____
other _____

Total Income _____

Expenses

taxes (estimated
  Fed., state, and
  FICA) _____
property taxes _____
investments _____
retirement savings _____
savings _____
insurance (life) _____
insurance (health) _____
insurance (auto) _____
insurance
  (homeowners) _____
insurance (other) _____

medical
  (doctor, drugs) _____
dental _____
food (groceries) _____
food (meals out) _____
utilities _____
telephone _____
credit card
  payments _____
loan _____ _____
loan _____ _____
childcare _____
education _____
subscriptions _____
clothing _____
cleaning _____
recreation _____
vacation _____
gifts _____
donations _____
grooming,
  personal care _____
auto (payments) _____
auto (gas, oil,
  maintenance) _____
other _____
other _____
other _____

Total Expenses _____

Now, here's the hard part: subtract your total expenses from your total income. This tells you where you have been in managing your cash flow.

Where you will want to be during this period is living within your income, ideally without drawing on savings or even a severance package. Having that cushion to fall back on should hard times continue goes a long way toward providing financial peace of mind. It's easier to "use it up, wear it out; make it do or do without"—to quote an old Yankee maxim—when you know that you won't have to live that way forever. (Then again, some people find that frugal living serves them better in the end anyway, and they never return to the same level of consumption they had before their job crisis.)

Living within your reduced income means two things: cutting back and earning extra cash. If your children are older, involve them in these decisions. "The more children are involved in a decision, the better," says child psychiatrist Dr. Foster Cline. Remember, children like to be part of problem solving. And they will complain less when they feel they have some say in what they have to give up. Older kids can learn valuable lessons from having to earn their own spending money as well.

Some Ways to Cut Back

Some categories, obviously, are easier than others to cut back or cut out completely, but it's almost always possible to find ways to cut back on expenses. In fact, it's usually easier and more efficient to do this than it is to earn income. Many of the people I talked to have found some creative ways to pinch a penny.

Shop garage sales and resale shops. You can find inexpensive household items, furniture, clothing, almost anything from these sources. Even if you have style-conscious teenagers, resale shops can work. Carol and Mindy Falen would skim fashion magazines for what's "in," then they scoured the resale shops to put together outfits that even brought compliments from unsuspecting friends.

Put out the word. Let people know of your need, whether it's for clothing, school supplies for the kids, furniture, or large appliances. You don't have to ask anyone outright. Just say, "I'm looking for such and such. If you know of anyone who is willing to part with theirs for a good price or is willing to trade services, let me know."

Barter your services. This is a challenging and potentially endless way around a cash shortage. Locate someone whose services, wares, or information you need and in turn fill a need of theirs. One man approached an electrician who owned a horse ranch and offered to work on the ranch in exchange for some electrical work. The rancher needed his horse corral painted, and the two men made a deal. In a similar way, you could trade your garden vegetables for a neighbor's fruit. You could tutor a child in exchange for the father's services on your car. And on and on. Bartering takes courage to do, especially if you're used to paying cash for every service or product you want. But it's a time-honored way of doing business, and it allows you to "cash in" on the one thing you do have more of these days: time.

Explore all resources. Look at what you have and how you can better use it. I highly recommend the book and newsletter, each called *The Tightwad Gazette,* for tips on how to do this (see appendix B). Some examples would be: grow your own produce; make homemade gifts; clip and use coupons; recycle. Borrow books from the library that will help you learn how to do the things you used to pay others to do. Explore your community for free forms of entertainment.

Exploring all resources also applies to health care. Ask your social-service agency if any low-cost health clinics operate in your area, especially those offering services such as vaccinations for children. Ask your doctor if he or she would be willing to work on a sliding-scale basis until you get on your feet again. If he or she won't, call around to see if anyone else will. Medical care is not something you can afford to do without if you need it.

Expand your view of giving. Some people wonder if they should continue to give to charitable causes. This of, course, is a personal decision, based on your own values and convictions. I will say that several of the couples I talked to felt strongly that a tenth (the tithe) of whatever came in belonged to God, and they continued to give that tithe of whatever income they had. All those who continued this practice said they were glad they did. It was one of the things that Pam Grisweiler admired and affirmed in her husband during his unemployment. Another man told me, "I don't understand it. When I was unemployed, we continued to tithe, and somehow all the bills got paid. Now that I'm working again, we don't seem to have enough to pay the bills, and we stopped tithing. I guess we should start tithing again." We can take God at his word that he will provide.

On the other hand, we can give in ways besides money. Again, you may have time on your hands now, and that is an equally precious commodity. I don't think that God looks at what we give as much as how we give—what our heart's attitude is. Are we trusting that God will provide and grateful for what he has already given us? Out of that fullness, decide what and how to give. "For if the willingness is there, the gift is acceptable according to what one has, not according to what he does not have" (2 Cor. 8:12).

What Not to Cut

There's one thing you must not cut, even though it eats into your budget: insurance. You may be able to cut back some by converting whole-life policies to term insurance, for instance, but don't drop any kind of insurance completely.

Not only would you be wiped out should a disaster happen, but in some cases (as with automobile insurance) it's illegal not to carry it.

There are often ways to cut back on insurance. For instance, if you have several life-insurance policies, it will be cheaper to consolidate them into one policy. The best tack to take is to refigure your needs, then arrange to meet with your insurance agent to re-evaluate your situation. Ask if your life-insurance policy has any cash accumulation. If you have cash in the account, you may be able to apply it to the premium. If you carry term insurance (no cash buildup), see if you can pay it in monthly or quarterly installments instead of semiannually or annually, to stretch out the payments.

You may also find ways to cut back on automobile and property, casualty, homeowner's/renter's insurance. Consider raising the deductible to lower the premiums. Take the time to analyze your policies and shop around for the best deal. (If your car is more than five years old, and paid for, you might drop comprehensive and collision altogether.) Don't drop liability, however. One small accident can wipe you out, especially in these litigation-happy days.

Health insurance is also crucial, though in the U.S. it is growing beyond the affordability of some. I interviewed two families in Canada, one with five children, the other with six children, both headed by husbands who were not employed and wives who did not have outside jobs. As we talked about how they got by, I couldn't help thinking that they could not survive in this country, solely because of health-care costs. Not only is the insurance expensive, but any medicine, deductible, and your part of the co-insurance can easily eat up a large chunk of the monthly budget, especially if you have young children or if someone in the family has a chronic health problem. Nevertheless, do what's necessary to keep on an insurance plan. Until the current health-care system is revised, if you lose your insurance, you are gambling your family's health and your financial future. One relatively minor illness, especially if it's chronic, could render you ineligible for coverage with another company.

You may want to consider an alternative to conventional insurance: a group called the Christian Brotherhood Newsletter. Basically, this group of Christians agree to pay each other's medical bills. You subscribe to the newsletter, pay a monthly contribution, and if you have a qualified need, other subscribers will pay it. For more information, contact: Christian Brotherhood Newsletter, 127 Hazelwood Street, P.O. Box 832, Barberton, OH 44203-0832; 1-800-374-2562.

Ways to Earn Extra Cash

If after looking for every possible way to cut back, you still can't live on your current income, you'll need to find a way to raise some additional cash. Or you may have to resort to any or all of these measures if your job search continues longer than your savings and/or severance allows. Here are some suggestions for earning cash:

Self-employment. Reassess skills you may be able to market. The advantage of this is you set your hours (between your job search and interviews) and may find yourself tapping some rusty skills you forgot you enjoyed.

For years Jim Walters had been singing solos in his church. When he became unemployed, he called engaged couples and mortuaries, offering to sing at weddings and funerals. Soon he was performing at banquets, clubs, and civic affairs in addition to singing in churches. As a result of those contacts, he and his wife, Candace, enjoyed an all-expenses-paid trip to Florida, where Jim sang for a national convention.[4]

A variation of this is free-lance or consulting work. You may be able to hire out your services to former employers or clients on a project basis. The advantages are not only that you keep your hand in your field and keep in touch with people who may know of more permanent jobs, but also that you are continuing to be paid for your work. You may even find that this life suits you better, especially if you were near retirement anyway and secretly dreamed of cutting back. It may also be easier to call a contact and say, "I'm looking for work and wonder if your company ever hires out free-lance work" than to say, "I'm out of a job and wondered if you have an opening."

Temporary work. More and more companies are hiring "temps" in offices and factories. If you decide to explore this, contact an agency that does not charge you a fee; fees should be paid by the company doing the hiring. You may have skills that lend themselves to seasonal work—doing taxes, for instance. If you have a college degree, you may be able work as a substitute teacher; check with local school districts.

Part-time work. Restaurants, retail stores, and grocery stores may be good sources of part-time work. Some places provide benefits even if you don't work a thirty-five- or forty-hour week.

Unemployment insurance benefits. If you have lost your job, you may qualify for unemployment insurance. Check with your state to determine if you're qualified. This benefit is not welfare; it is something paid for by your employer. Go to your local unemployment or Job Service center. If you are unemployed and money is a problem, you owe it to yourself and your family to apply, even if you hate the idea of dealing with the state bureaucracy.

Retirement funds. If you have a distribution from your company retirement plan, it's best if you can transfer it to an Individual Retirement Account (IRA); in most cases you pay a 10 percent penalty for taking it as cash, plus you pay taxes on it. Unless you really need the cash, you're gambling your future to take it now in cash. Beware of a new trap, however:

you used to have 60 days in which to roll over the distribution into the IRA, but as of January 1, 1993, employers are required to collect 20 percent withholding tax from retirement-plan distributions paid out to individuals. If you initiate a rollover, you are still required to deposit the full amount of your plan payout into the IRA, including the amount withheld. This means you will have to pay, *out of your own pocket,* the 20 percent of the payout. So, if you take a $100,000 distribution, you will receive $80,000 after the $20,000 is withheld. To make a rollover, you must add $20,000 of your own to the $80,000 to be able to deposit $100,000 in the IRA within 60 days. The withheld tax may be refunded or applied against your other tax liabilities when you file your tax return.

To avoid withholding tax, make a trustee-to-trustee transfer of your plan distribution. Withholding does not apply to funds sent by the trustee of your retirement plan directly to the trustee of your IRA, without any amount being paid to you.[5]

Savings and investments. Besides the obvious savings accounts, you may have insurance policies that have cash value or savings bonds or other investments. Consider whether an investment is liquid—readily convertible to cash—or illiquid. Liquid investments include certificates of deposit, life-insurance cash values, stocks, bonds, savings bonds, and mutual funds. Carefully weigh the costs of liquidating your investments. Some, like certificates of deposit and bonds, carry a penalty. Stocks, bonds, and mutual funds may take a beating if the market conditions are poor for selling. Illiquid assets are those for which a market is not readily available. Real estate, business interests, or collectibles are examples of illiquid assets that may take a long time to liquidate and may not fetch an acceptable price.

It's wise, if conditions are not good for liquidating, to do so only for dire straits, such as keeping your health insurance or keeping your home from foreclosing. Look at other alternatives first.

Taking out a loan. Sometimes it's inevitable to need a loan from family or from a financial institution, but again, this is more of a last-resort option. If you borrow from family members, write out a contract of how much you are borrowing, when you will pay it back (within one year after obtaining full-time employment, for instance), and how much interest you will pay. The contract will let your family members know how serious you are about repaying, and it will help you keep your dignity.

Sell what you can. Hold a garage sale and get rid of whatever you can. Sell large items such as appliances or a second car through classified ads; contact local dealers for specialized collections. If you don't really need an item, put it on the selling block.

Other. Perhaps you have the space to rearrange an extra room and rent it out, or you could swap rent for childcare or household services. Perhaps you have other equipment (a seldom-used computer) that you can rent to a free-lance worker. Sit down with your family and perhaps even some creative friends and explore options you may not have considered.

Be sure to consider help from individuals, charitable organizations, or community groups. Many people I talked to said that other people or groups helped them with groceries (one family knew a butcher who regularly gave them meat; another family was periodically given groceries from a single church member who wanted to help), clothing, or cash for paying bills. Some people found help from their church in paying bills. It's hard to ask for help, of course. But many people who learn to do so during their time of need are then able to turn around and help others when they get back on their feet. As Norma Lorner told me, "You learn that it's a gift to others to sometimes let them minister to your needs."

Other social services are also available to you (see chapter 13). Do some research in the phone book to find the names and numbers of government agencies, your community's department of social services, and organizations such as the United Way, the Red Cross, and the Salvation Army.

A Word About Credit

During hard times, it's extremely tempting to use credit cards to get by. But know that you are digging a deeper hole for yourself each time that magnetic strip passes through a retailer's machine. Not only will you have to pay the price of the item, but you'll owe a hefty finance charge as well. If you can't afford to pay for the item with cash, you can't afford it. Many financial experts advise that you cut up your credit cards the first time you aren't able to pay the full balance each month.

If you have already bought consumer goods on credit, sell them if you possibly can to pay off the debt. For balances you can't pay off, pay only the monthly minimum. Always pay something, or your credit will be damaged. Contact those creditors you might have trouble paying. Some creditors will allow a month's grace period for missing a payment. But once you use it, it's gone, so use the opportunity only as a last resort.

Use your bank card only for emergencies, such as a car repair or a new refrigerator or new furnace if your old ones die.

If your bills become overwhelming, seek help through the Consumer Credit Counseling Service or other similar organizations, which offer low-cost (on a sliding scale) or no-cost confidential and professional counseling on money matters of all kinds. They will help you set up a budget, cope with your debts, and use credit wisely. If you are having trouble financially, especially if you're in debt, contacting a

Consumer Credit Counseling Service now could save you money, your credit rating, and even your home.

Step 4: Develop a Résumé

Many people mistakenly think writing a résumé is the first step. I believe it should wait at least until you've done your self-assessment. "Getting stuck in the 'mail mode'—where you just mail out lots and lots of résumés—is the kiss of death to a job search," said career counselor Karen Volpert. Résumés are used to screen people out, not in. Résumés are useful in helping you pinpoint your accomplishments, and most companies will ask you to give them one eventually. But once you write it, save it. Don't bring it out until the very end of the process. Then use it as a script in an interview.

What kind of résumé should you write? Several books can help you with this.[6] You really have lots of latitude. The only thing you can't do is lie or make up things you haven't done.

List at the top of your résumé the accomplishments that are most gratifying to you. It's most effective to use the P-A-R method: briefly state what the *problem* was, what *action* you took to deal with it, and the *results*. Use action verbs. At the bottom, under "Additional information," list your interest in backpacking or politics or whatever. This may seem unorthodox, but one counselor points out that additional information like this often provides the interviewer with an icebreaker and also offers clues for a potential employer to figure out whether you have anything in common. She also attests that she received three job offers that began because she admitted to an interest in dry fly fishing.

Step 5: Develop a Network

The vast majority of jobs are never advertised but filled through personal contacts. Most people find jobs by connecting with someone with whom they have an affinity—with whom they share a passion. This is the point at which you use the information you gleaned from your self-assessment, from discovering your "gifted passion." At this point you are looking for people who share your values and interests.

Start an affinity list. Include all the people you know and love—family members, children, best friends. Use your résumé to jog your memory about peers, consultants, vendors, people you supervised, and bosses. List everyone you can think of, then cross out the ones you disliked.

Now, call every person on your list. Ask the person to meet with you for twenty minutes to brainstorm with you about what's going on in their world. Plan to meet with as many people as you can in a day—at least three every day—for coffee, lunch, or breakfast.

Keep in mind that you're not meeting to ask for a job; you're meeting to talk about something that's of interest to you both. You may talk about who is developing new software systems or who has the most innovative techniques in corrugated packaging or what it takes to start a family-owned company. If the topic is compelling for you and if you know the other person shares your interest, you will have a stimulating conversation. You will leave a lasting impression on that person. He or she may not have room for you right now, but if a job that suits your gifts opens up, that person probably will remember you and will contact you about the job. And you will come out of your meeting with new ideas and other people to talk to.

Do not bring a résumé to these networking meetings. All that does is make the person think, "Oh no, he wants a job, and I don't know of any jobs." Then the person shuts down. You are not asking for a job; you are brainstorming. Your goal is to come away with two provocative new ideas about companies or special areas of interest and with the names of two or more people to add to your list. Call them.

This approach is a variation of the "information interview" that's so highly touted, but this approach goes a step beyond. What may happen is that as you talk with this person, you will most likely develop a rapport because you share some interest. As you talk, an idea may begin to form in the back of the other person's mind. He or she has sensed a vague need in his or her business, but it hasn't even jelled to the point where it's a recognizable job. But as you are provocative and informed and curious about the other person and his or her business problems, suddenly he or she sees in you the solution. The person may create a job then and there, even though none existed. Or the person may ask you to do a special project, and that may grow into a job. Focusing your job search in terms of shared values and rapport is even more effective than merely looking at function and industry.

Step 6: Keep Notes

Keep records of names, addresses, dates, and phone numbers of every person with whom you talk. (Note that job-search related expenses that exceed two percent of your adjusted gross income are tax-deductible—if you are looking for a position in your present field. This includes meals, long-distance calls, mileage to and from meetings, postage, stationery, job-search books, résumé services, and the like.)

Send thank-you notes after every conversation. "Thanks for meeting with me. I've talked to two of the people you suggested and am still trying to reach two others. Here's my business card. Let me know what I can do to return the favor." You may also include your résumé, if you like. But do include your business card; people are most likely to hang on to those.

You may also want to keep a record of other leads you have followed up, for instance from classified ads. Most career experts discourage people from spending too much time on job ads because most of the time those positions have already been filled by the time the ad runs. Even if they haven't, the company receives hundreds of résumés. If you want to work for the company that lists the ad, the best way is to make a contact with someone who works there and get introduced that way. "Never settle for a cold contact when you can reach a warm body," says Dave Swanson.

Step 7: Use Every Resource

You will find a wealth of resources about the various methods of job hunting. I list several of what I consider the best in appendix B. This chapter attempts to give you the kernel of the best methods. I urge you to assess what you need, what you lack, and how you can fill in the gaps.

Tell everyone you meet that you're looking for a job. One man told me that he stopped to help a man whose car was disabled, and as they talked, he mentioned he was looking for a job in advertising. It turned out the man was an artist who worked for several advertising firms. The man who stopped to perform a good deed left that night with a list of new contacts in some important advertising firms.

What about executive-search firms, outplacement services, recruiters, and career counselors? It depends on your field and your needs. In general, if your skills are in demand in an area, a recruiter or executive-search firm may help. If you don't know what you want to do, a career counselor might help. Beware of two dangers in using these kinds of services: they are not always that reputable, and you can fall into the trap of leaving your search in their hands. No career test will tell you what a thorough self-assessment can tell you. No recruiter can communicate your passion as well as you can when you're eyeball to eyeball with someone else who shares that passion. Check out the companies and use them if you feel they will help.[7] Just remember that you are the only one who will get yourself a job in the end.

Step 8: Prepare for Interviews

When your networking does result in an interview, prepare well for it. Research the company and its competitors. If you're applying to a major corporation, call the customer-relations department and ask for written material about the corporation. If the company is privately held, research the company at the public library or local chamber of commerce. And, of course, talk to anyone you know in the company to get a perspective not only on the company but also on the person who will interview you.

Hone your presentation skills. "Get one friend to conduct a mock interview and another to videotape it," advises Harvey Mackay, author of *Sharkproof: Get the Job You Want, Keep the Job You Love in Today's Frenzied Job Market.* "There's no substitute for an exercise like this because you see and hear your strong points and weak points. Do you have good posture? Do you say a lot of 'ah's' and 'er's'? Do your eyes float around the room, or do you maintain eye contact with the interviewer?"

Use your résumé as a script, focusing on your most impressive accomplishments and giving evidence of your best characteristics. Smile and develop a rapport. Look for the shared affinity mentioned earlier.

Finally, plot your follow-up strategy during the interview. Look for clues that hint at the interviewer's objections to you and either try to allay those fears then or do it later. For instance, one man prepared a newsletter for a prospective client to prove he could handle the public-relations duties of the job. Although he had no formal experience in public relations, he felt sure he could do it. He was hired for the position, in part because he had proven ahead of time, through the sample newsletter, that he could do the job.

Step 9: Persevere, Persevere, Persevere

Inoculate yourself against rejection. Remind yourself that "it's always too soon to quit." That next contact may be the lead to the job of your dreams. Someone you talked to eighteen months ago may finally have an opening that's just right for you. Exercise your faith that God is in control and that this is not punishment but preparation. Reread the story of Jesus feeding the five thousand (Luke 9:10–17; John 6:1–13). Did you notice that Jesus instructed the disciples to pick up what was left over so that "nothing [would] be wasted" (John 6:12)? God does not intend anything in our lives to be wasted either. Someday, I believe, you will look back and see how he has used each of your experiences to weave a tapestry of the unique pattern of his hand in your life.

Never give up. God has provided all you need to accomplish his purposes through your life. If you don't know what those are, pray to discern them. "If any of you lacks wisdom, he should ask God, who gives generously to all without finding fault, and it will be given to him" (James 1:5). God will open the doors and shed light on your path. It's your responsibility to go through the door, to take whatever the next step is for you.

I leave you with two encouraging passages:

Trust in the Lord with all your heart and lean not on your own understanding; in all your ways acknowledge him, and he will make your paths straight (Prov. 3:5–6).

Commit to the Lord whatever you do, and your plans will succeed (Prov. 16:3).

· 11 ·

Be a Supportive Spouse

If you are the wife of someone who is out of work, underemployed, or who hates his job, you can be his greatest source of encouragement. Vic Glavach underscores how important a wife's influence is: "When a husband is out of work and can't get an employer to even look at him, he feels terribly incapable. If a wife says, whether in actual words or just by her attitude, 'What's wrong? Why can't you get a job?'—he actually becomes more incapable."[1]

The first key to helping your husband through his crisis is to understand what he is going through. If you have managed to establish effective communication in your marriage, you will be able to talk about your feelings and observations. But some men find it difficult to share their deepest emotions, and sometimes it's best to give them their space to work things through themselves. Some men find it unhelpful to talk about their problems and feelings; to them it's equivalent to dwelling on the negative. Know your husband and his needs. If he hasn't been communicative, you will know from the early chapters of this book what he might be feeling, even if he doesn't express those feelings.

A second key to offering true help is to be committed to facing the situation as *partners*. Vic Glavach said his period of unemployment taught him what a symbiotic relationship in marriage is. Each spouse needs the other, and each spouse profoundly influences the other.

This is why one of the hardest things for most wives is the lack of control over the situation. "I'd almost rather it had happened to me instead of my husband," one wife said. "Then at least I'd feel in control." This perfectly natural desire for control can lead to some well-intentioned but dangerous actions.

HARMFUL ACTIONS

Offering Advice

You see something your husband should be doing, and you offer your advice—only to find that he discards it and even seems to resent it. What happened? When the wife introduces her advice when it isn't sought, her husband may doubt himself even more. He may wonder, *If I had done it her way, would I have a job by now?*

You want to be a part of his job search, yet it's important to maintain a balance between overinvolvement and indifference. On the one side is the temptation to try to control too much, which can interfere with both his job search and your relationship. Monitoring his job search, giving advice when it's not asked for, and attempting to control what he does only push you apart. Several men mentioned they dreaded their wives' daily, "So, how many interviews did you have today?" They felt their wives were checking on them; they felt like little boys, answering to Mama. One man said the question felt like a daily curse.

On the other hand, total lack of involvement may look like lack of support to your husband. The best way to find the balance that works for you and your husband is to say something like, "I really want to help you in your job search. What can I do for you?" Let him tell you what he would like you to do for and with him. If he's not sure, you might make suggestions and see how he responds: "Would you like me to have lunch with some of my friends and see if they know anyone in your field you can talk to? Would it help if I typed up your cover letters or résumé?" Getting involved in ways he feels are helpful will both communicate your support and yet acknowledge that he is ultimately responsible for getting himself a satisfying job.

Misguided Support

Is it possible to be *too* supportive? Probably not. But it is possible to "support" in a misguided way, by picking up too much of the slack. Really, it's just a more subtle form of control, in which the support person carries not only her own load but his as well.

The weaker person may actually encourage the stronger person to carry the full load. Kerry Marone said, "One time Bob told me he felt he was drowning, and I was on the shore and wouldn't throw him the life preserver." The "life preserver" in that case was consenting to move to Florida. Bob thought he would feel less depressed in the warmer, sunnier climate. Kerry had even gotten a good job offer down there. But she thought Bob was basing his salvation on an outward situation—where he lived—and she was reluctant to give up her support system at home. "Bob was trying to put me back into a role I was trying to get out of," she said—the role of pulling all the weight, of doing for Bob what he should be doing for himself. "The rules in our relationship were changing. I knew we would either have a stronger marriage or things would fall apart. He was getting weaker, and then I would control. Seeing where I was going, I would then pull back." Kerry slowly learned a hard lesson: that in order to help Bob best, she had to let go of some things, let him make some of his own decisions and mistakes, while she attended to some of her own needs. She found that somehow, by letting go, she freed Bob to become his own person.

I also had to learn that growth comes for both husband and wife when the wife steps back and lets the husband do whatever hard work he has to do to cope with and come to terms with his situation. When Gene thought he wanted to enter a doctoral program, I said I supported his desire. It would mean moving down to a state I knew I would dislike and giving up a job I loved. But I was willing to make those sacrifices, with one condition: that he finance his end of it. I would not, could not, take on all the financial responsibility for our family. I didn't think it would be healthy for me to do so. I knew the desire and motivation to get through a rigorous program would have to come from within him. And it would have to be strong. The proof of whether he had that strong motivation would be for him to find a way to make it work, I felt.

There was a time in our marriage when I would not have set that condition. I would have moved, found a way to support us both, and put him through school in an attempt to be "supportive." And I would later have resented it deeply. My picking up all the slack doesn't help either one of us. We realized that the hard way. Now Gene tells me to butt out when I'm doing too much!

Blaming

If there is one danger you must guard against at all costs, it is blame. Blame is poison—to you, to the relationship, to your husband's attempts to move forward. Perhaps you have legitimate reasons to blame your husband. Maybe, like Derek Halstad, he turned down a secure job to work for a ministry that would "make a difference for the Lord," but now he is out of a job. Perhaps he jumped into an expensive and time-consuming graduate program in an obscure field, without considering whether there were any good prospects of employment in his field. Perhaps he made some mistakes and lost a business. As time wears on and you ride the emotional roller coaster together, you can't help but think of all the things your husband should have done to avoid your current situation. Worse yet, you may have pushed him to leave the company before the situation got worse, but he chose to stay.

Perhaps this need to blame is also tied to the lack of control wives feel. If only we knew whom to blame, we could at least pinpoint the source of our distress. In a marriage undergoing the stress of a job crisis, it's hard to know whom to blame. So we turn *against* each other, instead of *toward* each other.

Everyone has regrets about career choices. If recurring thoughts of "I told you so" or bitterness eat away at you, deal with them now. Realize that you are only hurting yourself by hanging on to blame.

Betsey Glavach found herself most tempted to lash out and blame Vic for their situation during the time they were trying to sell their house. Knowing that a realtor could call any minute and ask to show the house in half an hour wore on her. She said, "That constant strain of keeping things perfect got to me. It was when I was constantly cleaning and straightening the house that I'd feel the most like lashing out and wanting to blame Vic. But whenever those feelings hit me, I would get this clear picture in my mind that striking out at Vic would be like shooting myself in the foot. If I dumped on him, he'd be less capable of helping and encouraging me. We knew we needed that mutual support, and neither of us wanted to do anything to destroy that."[2]

Betsey knew that turning against rather than toward her husband would have been devastating. A husband in a job crisis already experiences self-doubt. If his wife also doubts him at this time and blames him for their situation, it can demoralize him and tear apart the marriage.

Wives can't change the situation, but we can choose how to respond. Two Scripture passages may help. Ephesians 4:31 instructs us to "Get rid of all bitterness, rage and anger" and verse 32 tells us how: "Be kind and compassionate to one another, forgiving each other, just as in Christ God forgave you." The more I focused on my own failures and how Christ has forgiven me, the more I was able to forgive Gene and be compassionate. Philippians 3:13–14 also speaks to the husband and wife in a job crisis. Paul says, "But one thing I do: Forgetting what is behind and straining toward what is ahead, I press on toward the goal to win the prize for which God has called me heavenward in Christ Jesus." Godly living is our prize and our goal, and part of that is showing compassion and support to the husbands who need us now.

WHAT YOU CAN DO TO HELP

As a wife, you are in a unique position to give your husband emotional as well as practical support. Each marriage, each job crisis is different, so find ways that make sense in your situation.

Provide Emotional Support

Perhaps one of the most important ways you can support your husband during this stressful time is giving him emotional encouragement and strength.

Remain loyal to your husband. When people make cutting remarks about your husband's situation, remain loyal to him and defend him. Wives have told me that relatives or friends have told them that their husbands should "shape up," that their husbands were "shirking their duty," that their husbands should "take any job that came along," that their husbands were sinning, that the wives should give their husbands "a good swift kick in the pants." People are often full of advice and opinions. Sometimes their opinions express some of your own feelings or fuel your doubts.

I believe you need to cut off all such remarks and defend your husband. Doing so reinforces your own commitment and lets people know that they have overstepped a boundary into your business. One man told his wife to say to people, "If you have anything to say about my husband, please say it to him directly."

Don't let other people, especially your family, bad-mouth your husband. Too many wives have told me that others' remarks have damaged their marriage. One sad case involved a husband who knew that his wife was agreeing with some of the derogatory remarks being made about him. He lost trust in his wife, and their marriage is headed for divorce.

Listen. This may be the biggest need men have. Although it's true that some men prefer not to talk about what they're feeling, most find they feel better if they can express themselves to their wives without fear of censure. Vic said, "A couple of times I felt despair about our relationship because I felt I couldn't be totally open about my own feelings without distressing Betsey. We talked about that, and I told her how I needed to be able to talk to her, that if I couldn't talk to her I couldn't talk to anyone."[3] That's probably true for most men: if they can't talk to their wives, they don't feel they can talk to anyone. Vic knew Betsey's support for him was solid when he started to fall apart emotionally. "She just held on and encouraged me. She proved I could depend on her—even at my lowest point."[4] That gift of proven dependability is one of the choice treasures that can emerge from the crucible of your crisis.

Be a reality check. Your husband's emotions will tend to skew how he sees himself and everything that happens.

Remind your husband (and perhaps yourself) of the things he has done well in the past. Communicate your beliefs in his abilities. During a job crisis, men can easily lose sight of their own strengths.

You can also help your spouse know when to be patient and when not to be. For example, if a prospective employer said he would get back to him in a week and several weeks have passed, you can remind him that while a day might seem like a week to him, the reverse may be true for those on the other side of the hiring table.

Providing a reality check may also involve loving confrontation at times. If all your husband has been doing for the past week is lying on the couch watching television, and you're getting more and more uptight, talk to him about it. "Honey, I can't help but notice you haven't done anything with your job search. That makes me feel very anxious and worried. What's going on?" Then listen. He is blocked somehow, and your listening ear may help him work through the block.

Help him feel needed. Because your spouse is more fragile at this time, you may want to protect him. But don't treat him as if he's an invalid or incompetent simply because his work life isn't in place. He needs to feel needed, perhaps now more than ever. Don't be afraid to look to your spouse for the kind of advice, support, and practical help you normally sought from him.

Don't be afraid that you are adding to his burden when you ask for counsel and opinions. More than likely, your husband will welcome the chance to feel needed. If you had a lousy day at work or with the kids, don't be afraid to say, "I really had a rough day. May I talk to you about it?" Rather than see your request as a burden, your spouse may receive it as a chance to help solve a problem and forget about his own job-search worries for a while.

Again, it comes down to knowing your spouse, and

maintaining open communication. If when you share your problem he does seem burdened, ask him about it. "You seem impatient, as if you don't want to listen. What's going on?" He may admit that your work problem only reinforces that he doesn't have a job. You can then point out that he always gave you such valuable input in the past and that not having a job doesn't negate his past experience in the work world. Listen and accept his feelings, but also provide that reality check. You still need him, and he still has much to offer.

Offer the comfort of your love. Your husband needs your love most right now. Learn your husband's "love language"— what makes him feel most loved and accepted. Dr. Gary Chapman, author of *The Five Love Languages,* suggests five "languages" that communicate love: touch, words of affirmation, acts of service, giving gifts, and spending quality time. If you aren't sure what makes your husband feel loved, ask him which of these five things makes him feel most loved and nurtured. Dr. Chapman suggests that everyone has a primary and secondary love language. Once you know what your husband's are, you can practice them as the primary means of communicating your love and support.

If his primary love language is "acts of service," find out what you can do for his job search. If his love language is "words of affirmation," seek every opportunity to praise him and remind him of his strengths. If his language is touch or spending time together, make the most of the extra time he has on his hands. Even if your spouse's love language is "giving gifts" and you have no money, you can still be creative. Tina Waters, whose husband worked a stressful job he hated, would slip into his lunch a note or a picture that one of the children drew, to remind him that they loved him no matter what. She found ways to give "gifts from the heart" even though she had no money to spend. Her loving tokens of encouragement did a lot to strengthen her husband's ability to deal with a stressful situation.

Encourage him. Whether he hates his current job or is unemployed and looking for work, your husband faces continual rejection and discouragement. The world is tearing him down daily. Someone has said it takes twenty-five positive strokes to overcome one negative blow to one's self-esteem. The point is that your husband needs your praise and encouragement, as much as you can dish out. He needs to be reassured often that you believe in him. As Vic Glavach said, wives need to realize that they have a direct effect on the ability of their husbands to find a job. "Your encouragement can make all the difference."

But what if your belief in your husband has slipped? What if you're mired in your own worries and stresses brought on by this crisis that you didn't choose and can't control? Avoiding blame, curbing the need to control while at the same time being involved in his job search, encouraging, defending, and comforting your husband—these things can seem overwhelming when you wrestle with worries and stresses of your own. So how can you become the encourager your spouse needs?

First take care of your own needs and find a place to vent your own feelings. In order to be strong enough to give your husband the support he needs, you need to concentrate on getting your own needs met as well.

Take Care of Yourself

You are a whole person, with physical, emotional, mental, social, and spiritual needs. Taking care of yourself during your husband's job crisis means attending to all these areas.

Take care of yourself physically. Eat a low-fat diet with plenty of fruits and vegetables. Get enough rest and exercise. In other words, take all the recommended precautions for handling stress.

Take care of yourself emotionally. Find someone with whom you talk freely, knowing that the person will listen empathetically without judging you or your husband. You need to have someone—besides your husband—on whom you can lean for support because sometimes he will have nothing to give. Besides, you need someone to give you "reality checks." If you feel a spouse support group would help you, read chapter 12 for ideas about how to find or start one.

Take care of yourself mentally. Your husband needs you to be positive most of the time. But if you're having a hard time staying positive, you need to work on that first. Look at whatever trips you up and work on it. If you're having a hard time seeing your husband's strengths, for instance, pray for God to open your eyes. Then sit down and draw up a list of every strength, every little thing you appreciate. Look over your list every day.

Focus on the problem, not the person. Remind yourself that it's the job situation, not you, that is causing his grumpiness or lack of energy. Adjust your expectations accordingly.

Taking care of yourself mentally also involves taking mental breaks from your worry. What can you do to take your mind off your problems? If you had or have a career, this may offer a welcome respite. For other women, a class, volunteer work, or a hobby might take their minds off their problems for a time.

Take care of yourself socially. Now is not the time to "hide out." Try to keep up your normal contacts, if possible. You may need to identify those few people who understand and accept you as a couple and to deepen those relationships. But do make sure you have people with whom you can have fun, with whom you can share some personal goals.

Take care of yourself spiritually. Daily focus on God and the fact that he is in control of the situation. Some women also find it helpful to record their thoughts and feelings in a journal.

"Sometimes it just comes down to this: pray and let God work," one woman told me. Pray for your husband and your situation. It's even better if you have the prayer support of at least one other person. Career counselor Richard Hagstrom recommends asking a small group of people to pray regularly for the job situation.

Getting the support you need first will give you the resources you need to provide not only the needed emotional support but also the practical support that can turn around your situation.

Provide Practical Support

Emotional support is crucial, but you can also offer other kinds of support to your husband. Remember to let him take the initiative. Your job is not to steer but to sit in the passenger's seat and offer perspective and point out things that he might not see because he is driving.

You and your husband may want to put into writing what your collective goals are. You can each then specify what your individual responsibilities will be.

One collective goal undoubtedly will be financial. Perhaps you agree not to get into debt. If you both understand the financial picture and both agree on what you can and can't do without, you will avoid many arguments. You may readjust your plan as you go along, but if you communicate at the start and keep communicating, you will lessen the friction.

Another collective goal might be to maintain normal routines whenever possible. Discuss ways that you both can reduce stress.

Here are some of the possible things you can do to help in each step of the job search:

Allow a brief moratorium or grace period during which your husband can consolidate a new identity. Understand that the first few days or even the first two weeks of unemployment will leave your husband feeling at loose ends. Suggest that he get away from the job search to take some time to regroup. His goal for this time is to come away with a clearer sense of who he is and what he wants. It's a time to work through any of the emotions that are hindering his job search.

Help your husband identify his strengths. The method outlined in appendix A works best if two people work together. If your husband is open to it, interview him about his positive experiences and help him analyze the data for recurring patterns.

Encourage your husband to keep a progress log. Organization is important in a job search. Encourage your husband to keep a list of names, addresses, and phone numbers of contacts as well as what transpired in the phone call, correspondence, or interview. If he is comfortable letting you see his log, you can keep abreast of his efforts without having to ask him every day what he did. Rather than asking, "How many interviews did you have today?" keep your question open ended: "How did things go today?" or "How are you feeling now?" The key is to find a way to communicate so that you feel informed and so that he doesn't feel badgered.

Help your husband research jobs. If your husband would like help in the research part of the job search, you might do some of the legwork at the library or chamber of commerce. Of course, he's the one who will have to digest the information. But you might be able to help uncover some of it through making phone calls to the public relations department of a company, for instance.

Encourage your husband to relate to other men. Vic Glavach felt grateful that Betsey urged him to take time for relationships with male friends. "I got a lot of encouragement from those relationships," he said, "but Betsey would point out what I was doing and the benefits it had on the other people as well. That gave me a sense of worth."[5]

Help your husband hone his interview skills. Ask your husband to list the questions he most fears an interviewer will ask, and role play with him. You might even tape the session or ask a friend or one of the kids to tape the sessions.

Praise your husband daily. It bears repeating: many men feel inadequate, especially when they lose their jobs or work in jobs that don't match their abilities. When they're facing dissatisfaction or rejection daily, their self-esteem takes a battering. What they crave from their wives is praise.

What can you find in your husband to praise? Perhaps it's the fact that though he hates his job, he gets up every day and goes to work anyway. You can tell him how much you appreciate the strength he shows in doing this. Or maybe you appreciate and admire the way he's kept such an upbeat attitude, even in the face of discouraging results. If he displays weakness, let him know how honored you feel that he can open up to you about his true feelings. Whatever you can affirm, do it. Often!

Do some networking yourself—even if you're not currently involved in the business world. "We find that women who have never worked have little idea of the potential strength of their own networking," say Madelein and Robert Swain, authors of *Out of the Organization: Gaining the Competitive Edge*. "These women may be astonished at how many people they know well enough to call for lunch: family; a college roommate who might just know something about the husband's field; fellow volunteers; church or synagogue members; bridge partners; doctors; accountants—the list is limited only by the imagination of the spouse." And obviously if you are employed, you have another whole network to add to that list. The best approach, the Swains say, is a purposeful, unapologetic approach to your own circle of friends and acquaintances. Let them know what your husband is looking for and ask if they know of anyone your husband can talk to, not necessarily to get a job but to ask questions about the companies in which your friends are involved.

Initiate rewards and celebrations for goals achieved. This is one good reason to keep abreast of what's happening with your husband's job search. You may be able to see something that he doesn't. "You found a contact in that company you were interested in. Great! Let's celebrate!" He may reply that nothing's sure yet, the person didn't even agree yet to see him. No matter. If he's been trying to get the name of an actual person in a company he's interested in, and now he's got that name, that's cause enough to celebrate.

Even when things are not going well, suggest ways to take a break from the strain and have some simple fun. And don't forget that a sense of humor is a great weapon—some days, your only weapon—in your battle to gain a sense of control. Make it your goal to make your spouse laugh at least once a day. Rent a zany comedy. Make a "Top 10 List" of the favorite management blunders you have heard about. Imitate the dumbest responses you heard when telling others about your job crisis.

As you work together on a plan of action, tread gently. Remember these words of Vic Glavach: "Most people are good at telling other people what they ought to do. But that's not usually what we weak, hurting people need to hear. What we need is for someone to say, 'I know what you can do. You are able. You're on the right track.' Betsey did that for me." I'm confident you can do that for your husband as well.

· 12 ·

Find or Start
Support Groups

One of the best ways to combat feelings of shame and embarrassment over losing your job is to talk to others who have suffered the same fate," says Kathleen Riehle, author of *What Smart People Do When Losing Their Jobs.* Whether you lost your job or are looking to change careers or whether you are the spouse of a person in a job crisis, support groups offer moral support, networking opportunities, accountability, and understanding. Support groups can provide a peer group apart from family and friends. Many groups also provide training in job-search skills, ranging from putting your résumé together to making cold calls to negotiating a salary and benefits package once you land a job offer. My experience and the experience of others indicate that you can't afford to be without a support group of some kind if you're going through a job crisis.

Some men shy away from support groups because they have a mistaken notion of what happens there. One man told me, "I'm not interested in sitting down and having a pity party with other employed people—that would be pretty depressing." Yes, it would be, if that's all that happened. A good support group, however, doesn't degenerate into this. It's a place for people to talk about not only their fears and discouragement but also what they're doing about it. It's a place for people to hear from others who have weathered that storm and have come out on the other side.

In attending a support group for unemployed people at a large church, I was struck by the instant camaraderie that existed between people. After the speaker talked about handling the emotions of a career transition, people came up to each other and shared their stories of how long they had been unemployed and the feelings they had. After airing their feelings, talk inevitably turned toward helping each other: "I know someone in the airline industry. I'll be happy to give her a call for you." "I saw an article about your field in a business journal just last week. It might be worth a try to call the author and see if he has any leads." The men were encouraging not only each other but themselves as well: they still knew people; they still had something to give the world.

This chapter will look at what various support groups have to offer and how to find what you need. In case you are not able to find a group that meets your needs, this chapter also explores several successful group models that will help you start your own group.

HOW TO FIND A SUPPORT GROUP

Support groups for people looking for work are springing up all over in churches and communities. For instance, the metropolitan Chicago area alone has over fifty support groups of various kinds. Many of these groups are held in churches, and many offer high-quality outplacement services at little or no fee.

Before you look for a support group, take stock of what you need. Moral and emotional support? Support as the spouse? Networking opportunities? Training in job-search techniques? All of the above?

Most likely you'll want both support and some sort of help with job-search skills unless your company has already offered you outplacement services. The emotional support you need is different from the support you need to further your job search. Both are important, and I suggest you find ways to get both kinds of support. If you find yourself immobilized or isolated, a support group (or counseling) may help you deal with issues that can hamper your job search if you don't deal with them.

On the other hand, the problems of career trauma often stem from the condition itself. The answer, then, is to get at the problem, not the symptoms. If you have to err in one direction, I suggest you look first for a group that will offer practical training in job-finding techniques. This will help you attack the primary problem. If, after getting a satisfactory job, you still feel haunted by your emotions and experiences, you can see a therapist to work through your other issues.

Most of the more successful support groups have found that people respond best to groups that include a practical element. It's easier to tell people, "I'm going to hear an outplacement expert talk about how to develop a network most effectively" than to say, "I'm meeting with my unemployment support group." Positive action is one of the best things you can do to help yourself move along. Researchers have found that problem-focused coping—for example, seeking a new job or getting retrained in a new occupation—is more effective than simply trying to alleviate the depression or loneliness that comes with a job crisis. In effective support groups, both needs are satisfied. Like the group I visited, people will offer each other moral support and practical help naturally as long as the group allows time to do so.

If you are the spouse of someone going through a job crisis, you need a support group that offers moral and emotional support. The job search is up to your spouse. But you need a place to vent your feelings and be with others who have been or are going through the same thing.

Where to Find Support Groups

Where can you find support groups? Start with the churches and synagogues in your area, especially large churches or churches that are known for social outreach. Ask them if they have or know about a ministry to those looking for work. Many times several churches in an area pool their resources for an interdenominational ministry to the unemployed.

Some cities have job clubs, like Forty-Plus Clubs, Five O'clock Clubs (currently in New York City, but expanding to other cities), and Experience Unlimited Clubs. Most of these clubs charge membership fees, which for some clubs includes an office as a base for the job hunt as well as the use of computers, phones, fax and copy machines. Some communities offer job clubs that give emotional support as well as teach job-search skills.

Other places to contact for support groups and help in the job search are:

Social-service agencies
Business librarian at local library
Local unemployment center
YWCA, YMCA, YMHA, or YWHA
Chamber of commerce
Newspaper's business editor or librarian
Human-resources department of former employer
Local college counseling center
*National Business Employment Weekly**

---

*This publication is available at some newsstands, or you can order it directly from: *National Business Employment Weekly*, 420 Lexington Avenue, New York, NY 10170, (212) 808-6792 or 1-800-JOB-HUNT.

Characteristics of Successful Support Groups

What makes a support group effective? The following list describes characteristics you may want to look for in choosing a group or in starting one of your own.

Clear purpose. The group should know what its purpose is. For instance, the Career Resource Center, a coalition supported by thirteen churches in Chicago's North Shore area, adopted the following mission statement: "To provide spiritual, psychological, and technical help on an ecumenical basis to people seeking employment." They operate essentially as a non-profit outplacement agency, and they publicize their services to both job seekers and employers.

The groups that provide training in job-finding skills often have a set curriculum. For instance, the Interfaith Re-Employment Group in Pittsburgh, Pennsylvania, offers a four-week series on how to get an interview and a five-week series on how to prepare for and take an interview. Other seminars focus on coping with job loss and stress, legal rights of the unemployed, successful negotiating, and other topics. Other groups may add such topics as self-assessment, handling rejection, even dress-for-success techniques.

Some groups limit themselves to addressing emotional needs. These groups offer an important adjunct to the job-skills support groups. They depend on employed people who have gone through job crisis themselves to provide encouragement, accountability, and hope to the job seeker.

Positive focus. The most successful groups are not a gripe session but an opportunity to air frustrations and move on to positive action. These groups often have a facilitator who is trained to recognize when someone needs more help and who can refer a person to that help. When you evaluate a group, find out what kind of training the leader has had.

Free services. Although some clubs charge fees, many don't. Check out the free sources first. Many non-profit groups provide services that rival the best outplacement agencies, with professional outplacement and human-resources people volunteering their time and talents.

Connection with resources. Most support groups will give job seekers lists of books and other resources for the job hunt. Some even offer the use of a computer, photocopier, and fax machine. Many also provide a professional, one-on-one résumé critique and may videotape a practice interview. All should have knowledgeable people who can steer you toward the resources you need.

Trust. Groups whose purpose is to provide emotional support must promote trust and confidentiality. People will share deeply only when they know their feelings and perspective will be received with understanding and respect. Some spouse support groups tell their members not to talk about who attends the group because that can become a source of gossip. Confidentiality must be a hallmark of the group.

Dependable structure. The group should always meet at a set time and place, for a set period. By its very nature, such a group will be in flux: people will leave the group once they find a job. For the sake of the group's dependability many groups require that people who get jobs continue to attend the group to encourage those who are still looking. If you decide to start your own group, try to link up with an employed person who is willing to help. The group needs continuity if it's to grow and provide help.

Networking source. At the very least, the group should encourage and provide opportunities for members to share job leads with each other. Some of the best groups put your name and résumé information into a data base, which they then make available to employers. Some churches make available résumé directories and urge parishioners to get in touch with the people listed if they know of any job leads. Other churches ask parishioners to be resources to people seeking information about their field. The church's job club screens people to ensure that no volunteer receives more than two calls per month. The resource people help the job seeker understand more about that particular field and to provide the names of other people to whom the job seeker can talk. Job seekers are not allowed to ask resource people for jobs so that the resource people don't feel obligated to deliver more than they can.

SUPPORT GROUP MODELS THAT WORK

Before you begin to look for a support group or before you *start* a support group, let's examine several support group models: mentoring, emotional support, spouse support, outplacement, data base, job club.

Mentoring: Career Renewal Program

Career Renewal began in 1986 at Holy Cross Catholic Church in Deerfield, Illinois, by four parishioners who identified a need to support unemployed people. The plan was to provide a "friend/advisor" who would volunteer his or her personal strengths and skills not only to support the participant emotionally but also to assist in networking, career guidance, résumé development, caring, and understanding.

In 1989, after assisting a participant from nearby St. Gregory's Episcopal Church, four members of St. Gregory's became advisors. The two churches have worked together ever since in a joint venture.

Career Renewal holds meetings every two months, on a Sunday, at the Holy Cross Parish Center. The first hour, from 9:15–10:15 A.M., they hold an advisor or staff meeting. From 10:15 until noon they hold a workshop for the unemployed, during which they will match participants up with an advisor. These meetings are publicized through church bulletin inserts and through word of mouth. Career Renewal requests people

Advisors in Career Renewal are expected

- to become a partner with the participant throughout the term of the job search.
- to call a participant at least once every three weeks to check the participant's status.
- to be aware of other programs and resources for job seekers (tapes, books, job fairs).
- to be aware of qualifications of fellow advisors in order to refer participants for further networking and counsel.
- to be aware of effective job-search strategies.
- to commit to both giving and receiving support.

Participants in Career Renewal are expected

- to take advantage of the programs and systems to the fullest extent possible.
- to forward their resúmé to each advisor.
- to share job leads with the group.
- to maintain bi-weekly contact with the advisor.
- to notify his or her advisor immediately on accepting a job opportunity.
- to consider volunteering as an advisor in the Career Renewal Program after his or her time as a participant.

to come with copies of their current résumé or if possible to forward a résumé ahead of time to a contact person.

While Career Renewal doesn't promise employment, they have had success. As of January, 1993, the group had thirty-seven advisors, with nearly all occupational disciplines represented. At that time they were assisting eighty-two unemployed participants from the Deerfield area. In 1991, thirty-four participants found employment, and in 1992 forty-seven became employed. Career Renewal also helps other churches start similar programs in their area.

CONTACT
Ronald J. Moskal
Career Renewal Program
316 Redwing
Deerfield, IL 60015

Emotional Support: The 59:59 Groups

The first 59:59 group was started as a care group by two men in Marietta, Georgia. In the words of one of the founders: "It was during a men's Bible study group in July 1991, that Darrell (not his real name) interrupted and said, 'There's something wrong here. You talk about Christian things, but it seems to me that many of you leave your Christianity at the door when you leave.' Darrell's statement bothered me, so I phoned him later that day and asked if we could meet the next morning for breakfast. Darrell wanted to tell me what he meant, so he agreed.

"At breakfast, Darrell explained to me that the recession had really hit his construction business hard. Bankruptcy was inevitable. The stress was causing severe problems at home. Darrell's fourteen-year-old son by a previous marriage had left in anger to live with his mother; communication with his wife was brittle and without love or understanding. Darrell's life was coming apart at the seams. I sat there, listening, not knowing what I could do.

"The following week I returned to the Bible study. It was there I learned that Darrell was found hanging in his home the night before. Dead to the world and dead to his Lord. We heard his call for help, and we waited for others—more qualified—to respond."

As Ray Brumbeloe and Jansen Chazanof discussed this tragedy, they both agreed that if only Darrell had received the help he so desperately called out for, the outcome might have been drastically different. Both Ray and Jansen had experienced career crises, and they discovered they had both made promises to themselves to help others overcome the problems they experienced. Now they felt they had to do something to prevent another tragedy like Darrell's.

After much talking, praying, and planning, the care group program called 59:59 began. Three or four employed people, preferably those who have experienced career trauma themselves, meet with three or four unemployed people for 59 minutes and 59 seconds. The purpose is to provide interaction, reinforcement, encouragement, candid appraisal, as well as individual and group accountability.

The group commits to staying together until *all* members of the group are gainfully employed; at which time the group may disband. The group has no leader; the responsibilities of conducting the weekly meetings revolve from one to the next, with no member excluded. Groups are either all male or all female, making it easier for people to share. One person is asked to be a "point person" to send and receive information from other 59:59 groups about job leads. But basically, 59:59 groups are "just friends helping friends through a difficult time." The Bible reference used as a foundation for 59:59 comes from 1 John 3:17: "If anyone has material possessions and sees his brother in need but has no pity on him, how can the love of God be in him?"

The 59:59 groups provide a free handbook that outlines its program. Of course, each group will take on the particular dynamics of the people involved, but the plan is a sound one and the potential for much support is great.

CONTACT
59:59 Career Support Groups
955 Johnson Ferry Road
Marietta, GA 30068
(404) 303-5959 (Voice Mail)
(404) 612-7577 (Hotline Voice Mail, for churches)

Spouse Support Group

One church has sponsored a very successful spouse support group, which then served as a catalyst to reach the husbands who were experiencing career trauma. That church has asked to remain anonymous because part of what makes it successful, says one of the founders, is its confidentiality. The church is located in an affluent suburb of a large city, where there is a great stigma attached to being unemployed. My contact told me, "People think that because we are in a wealthy community we have tons of money and great jobs and no problems—and none of this is true. We just have bigger problems and bigger bills if we undergo a career crisis."

This particular group was also founded by two men who had lost top-level jobs, felt they were given the cold shoulder by other Christians in the community, and wanted to do something about it once they found jobs. They formed a committee within the church to research and decide how best to reach their particular parish.

Because the stigma of unemployment was so high in this community of successful executives, the church felt it needed a back-door approach. The spouses of those men facing career problems were invited to a book discussion group. Other women who had been through something similar were also invited. The group studied a book on how career stress affects wives, which opened the way to much mutual support. The women also went home and talked about the book with their husbands, thus opening up communication about their painful experience.

Then the church started networking socials, inviting the women from the group, their spouses, and the career committee to a big barbecue. It was a "smashing success," and served to break the ice as men shared their stories with others.

From that group a ministry to the unemployed has blossomed, with meetings that feature speakers who discuss how to restructure skills to meet the demands of the current job market. But it all began when someone thought to reach out to the spouses and provide a way for wives to become the catalysts for husbands to deal with their crisis.

Another spouse support group has grown out of a community job club. The facilitator of the job club recognized a need for a support group for the spouses and started the wives' support group, which meets twice a month at a community center. At the support group, confidentiality is stressed. The spouses share what things have been like for them and help each other gain perspective on their feelings and brainstorm about solutions to problems. At the end of each meeting people exchange phone numbers so they can call each other between meetings if they need to talk. Again, for this or any group it is best to have a facilitator who is trained in group dynamics and who can provide stability for when people "graduate" from the group because their husbands have found jobs.

Outplacement: Willow Creek Community Church

Willow Creek Community Church's Careers Ministry was started in the early 1980s by two men who had been unemployed for around two years. It began as a support group in which people looking for work shared their experiences. Eventually, however, some of the people wanted something more; they wanted some practical help in finding a job. Rick Ehlers, director of Careers Ministry, says, "Some of the leaders asked, 'What else can we do or give these people so they can apply it immediately?' We developed a curriculum and philosophy of being almost an outplacement firm." While they could not provide office space for job seekers, as an outplacement firm does, they could provide the training, offered every Monday night.

The first training session deals with handling the emotions of the job search. Next they cover writing your résumé, marketing yourself through telemarketing, learning about various agencies, corresponding in writing, networking, and preparing for the interview. The Careers Ministry also deals with career transitions and negotiating salary and benefits packages. Members can sign up a week ahead for a half-hour, one-on-one consultation to work on career assessment, developing their résumé, and videotaping and reviewing practice interviews. Numerous handouts on the topic of the evening, resources, and other information are available at every meeting. A resource table offers books and tapes that participants can buy to help them with their job search. The church also offers a resource center containing a variety of books, magazines, articles, periodicals, and other reference materials available for people to review.

As the Careers Ministry evolved, it also added other services. They put together an assessment tool to help people determine the best direction to take. They contacted area companies and let them know of their ministry and asked for job listings they could post. They also have open meetings in which they might discuss whatever is on the minds of participants, or they might bring in someone to talk about image and appearance or how to handle finances during unemployment. They also developed an intensive two-day seminar with an accompanying manual that covered all the topics mentioned, plus a bibliography, resources, and Scripture references for encouragement and direction. They taped the workshop and make the video available to those who come to the Monday-night meetings. Careers Ministry has compiled a 147-page workbook called "The Creative Job Search Strategies Workbook," which outlines the content of their Monday night meetings and the longer, intensive workshop.

The Careers Ministry is led by a team of twenty people who come from a variety of backgrounds, especially human resources and counseling. They receive two or three months of training from Rick and the other leaders before they lead their sessions. Rick himself is a self-employed consultant who helps companies with internal career planning and development.

Willow Creek is an example of how one large church is garnering its resources to serve the needs of not only its own members but other churches as well. Its ministry evolved from a simple support group started by two men who themselves had experienced the agonies of a job search, to one that provides almost the same services as an outplacement agency would . . . at no charge.

CONTACT
Rick Ehlers
Careers Ministry
Willow Creek Community Church
67 E. Algonquin Road
South Barrington, IL 60010
(708) 765-5000

A program similar to Careers Ministry is Career Crossroads, another ministry run by a large church. Career Crossroads provides many of the services an outplacement agency does, at no charge, to members and those in the larger community. They sponsor job-finding seminars and weekly workshops that focus on key job-search skills. The leadership team includes a financial expert and a vocational counselor, as well as people trained to help with résumé writing, interviewing, and networking. Career Crossroads also lists participants in a data base they make available to employers in the area.

CONTACT
Karen Volpert
Career Crossroads
Church of the Savior
651 N. Wayne Avenue
Wayne, PA 19087
(215) 688-6302

Data Base: CEON

Christian Employment Opportunity Network (CEON) is currently based in the greater metropolitan Chicago area, but they are putting together a curriculum to help any group teach job-search skills and a seminar to develop leadership skills among church members. They are now primarily a computer data base that works in conjunction with churches that have (or are trying to start) a support group for people seeking work. Only churches may register applicants in the data bank, which means the church must have some sort of support team that is responsible for communicating with CEON. The church registers a thumbnail sketch of the person's résumé, which CEON makes available to employers searching for qualified candidates. The employers can then call the candidates to request a résumé or an interview.

Another way churches can participate is to encourage the

employers in the congregation to list job openings. Lloyd Bach, founder and director of CEON, feels that churches need to be made aware that employment struggles are widespread and that we need to minister to people's needs in this area. CEON makes available a monthly newsletter to subscribers and offers a brochure and information a church can use in its weekly bulletin to promote awareness of the problem and how people can become part of the solution.

Lloyd would like to expand the information base so that it can list other needs as well as job openings. For instance, someone may need a car to get to an interview; that can be listed, and a church tapping into the computer network can match the need with someone who can meet the need.

While CEON is seeking to expand to become a nation-wide network, they also serve as a model for other areas that may want to start something similar in their area.

CONTACT
Lloyd Bach
CEON
1255 Boa Trail
Carol Stream, IL 60188
(708) 837-8811

Non-church-based Job Clubs

Other job clubs are also available. One, which meets in several locations in the western suburbs of Chicago, is sponsored by the Lisle township and facilitated by Joy Dooley, who is employed by the township. The group, which meets in the public library, offers both moral support and specific help in job-finding skills.

The Lisle job club meets for two hours on a Friday

morning. The first part of the meeting is time for introductions; people state their names, what they are looking for, how their job search is going, and any leads or other information they want to pass on.

About halfway through the meeting, several people leave to meet with a retired outplacement specialist who donates his time to the club, helping participants hone their résumés. During the first part of the meeting, participants fill out a sign-up sheet with their name, address, phone number, and type of job they're looking for. During the break Dooley makes photocopies to distribute; people mill around, sharing information and encouraging one another.

After the break, someone trained in human resources gives a talk about some job-finding skill or technique. Afterward, people continue to linger, talking to one another. When a club member finds a job, the group celebrates with cookies and coffee while the now-employed person tells the group about the new job and how he or she found it. The atmosphere is upbeat, encouraging. Dooley also offers a spouse support group as well as one-on-one counseling and referrals. This is a local job club at its best, run by someone who has a vision for this and who is a trained facilitator. It is free of charge and open to all.

CONTACT
Joy Dooley
Lisle Township Youth Committee
5801 Westview Lane
Lisle, IL 60532
(708) 241-3237

Another kind of job club, the Forty-Plus Club of Chicago, addresses the needs of executives in search of work and is essentially an outplacement agency. It offers career assessment, résumé preparation, help in writing cover letters, and networking. The fee of several hundred dollars covers the cost of using the phones, computers, and office equipment. People who use the club's services feel as if they are going to work, which helps them keep focused. Forty-Plus Clubs stay in touch with employers seeking employees as well as with former Forty-Plus members who pass on job leads, so it is an excellent place to establish contacts. The main emphasis seems to be on job strategy, not support, although participants say that they do feel supported.

HOW TO START A SUPPORT GROUP

If you are unable to find a suitable support group and want to start one, either because you need one or because you have been through career trauma and would like to reach out to others, consider these steps.

1. Assess the Needs of Your Church and Community

Decide what kind of group you want to start—mentoring, emotional support, spouse support, outplacement, data base, job club. Whom do you wish to reach? Are they mostly white collar, blue collar, an even mix? Are there many single parents among the group? What kinds of resources already exist in your community? Do they mostly provide support, training in job-search skills, or a combination? Do the people in job crisis know about these resources? What do people seem to need most?

For example, if most of those in your congregation are already part of a small group and if you can assume they get support there, you may want to focus on providing job-search skills. On the other hand, there may be plenty of support for the unemployed, but nothing for spouses. Or the help may focus only on the unemployed and not the underemployed or those dissatisfied but stuck. Or you may want to reach out to community people who may not know where to turn in a job crisis. Talk to the leaders in your church and assess the needs of your congregation and community.

2. Get Support

You'll need at least one other person who will share your vision and help you get something organized. The person preferably should be employed, and it's ideal if he or she has been trained in the human-resources or social-services field. If you can't find a trained person right away, start with anyone who shares your vision. However, at some point you will need someone who has some training in group facilitating to keep the group on track.

Don't be afraid to start small. Remember, most of the ministries described in these chapters started with just two men. Pray, plan, talk to others, and pray and plan some more.

3. Formulate a Mission Statement

A mission statement will help you focus your vision as well as communicate it to others. A mission statement should describe what you are trying to do, whom you are trying to help, and how you will do it.

4. Gather Resource People

Depending on your goal, you may need many resource people or just a few. If you're starting a mentoring program, you will need as wide a group of resource people as possible. If you are starting a support group, it's best to balance unemployed with employed people, as the 59:59 groups do. If you want to start regular seminars to teach job-finding skills, line up people with human-resources and outplacement experience before you publicize your program.

5. Find a Place to Meet

You may want to meet at the church—many groups do. But then again, you may feel better about meeting in a public place, such as a library. Even if you plan to meet in a small support group, it's probably best not to meet in a home; that just entails an added burden of preparation each week.

6. Advertise the Meeting

You may wish to put a notice in your church bulletin several weeks ahead of the meeting. Or you may wish to send a letter to local churches, along with a request that they include the announcement in their bulletin. Or you may want to post an announcement in your local newspaper and send a press release. It all depends on your goal and whom you are trying to reach. It's best, however, to include the phone number of a contact person and ask for reservations so you have some idea of how many people to expect.

7. Hold Your Meeting

At the meeting, you may want to pass out handouts explaining who you are and what you want to offer. Ask attendees to fill out sheets with their name, address, phone number, the reason they're there, and kind of job they're looking for. State any ground rules that might apply. (For instance, if this is a support group, stress confidentiality and speaking only from their own experience—no advice giving. Other excellent guidelines are available from 59:59.) Pass out simple evaluation sheets so that you can get response on what was helpful, what didn't meet expectations. Encourage people to continue to interact with each other throughout the week. Networking is essential in the job search, and you have just provided them with new leads and potential contacts.

8. Evaluate and Fine-Tune Your Approach

Look over the evaluations and talk with your team about what you want to change as you go. Pray about direction; listen to the needs people express; then proceed boldly!

• 13 •

Tap Community
Resources

Jack and Mary Robinson didn't know where to turn. The business Jack had bought and built up had gone down the tubes. He faced not only bankruptcy but also unemployment. Because Jack had bought the business against Mary's wishes, severe tensions threatened to tear apart their marriage. No one in their church understood them or their situation. "Basically, we were treated like lepers," Mary said. Abandoned by friends and even family, hammered with stresses from without and within, things looked bleak for the Robinsons.

Then they heard about Turnaround Ministries, a group that helps people facing bankruptcy to get back on their feet spiritually and emotionally. Jack and Mary got involved and began to connect with people who both understood their needs and offered practical help in meeting some of them. When they got in touch with some resources available to serve their needs, the Robinsons discovered new hope and strength to carry on.

Whether your need is to get or stay out of debt, to learn job-search skills, to talk with potential employers, or to make ends meet financially, you will be able to find help. Ours is now an information- and service-based culture, which boasts an impressive array of opportunities for meeting people's needs.

FIND SERVICES TO MATCH YOUR NEEDS

What are your present needs? Make a list of everything that would help you in your job search, then prioritize the list. As you read through the following list of services, make a plan to get your needs met.

Financial Needs

If you need help paying your bills or feeding and clothing your family, swallow your pride and let people know you need help. Start close to home and branch outward from there. Let close family members know your problem. Go to your place of worship and let the staff know what your need is. Most churches and synagogues have ways of helping people in need. One man I know couldn't pay his mortgage one month during his unemployment, and the church paid it for him. Other people have received food, anonymous gifts of cash, clothing, furniture, and tickets for recreational events from their church. They were able to receive it as God's provision through his people.

Organizations like the United Way, the Red Cross, and Salvation Army also can help. Each of these organizations networks with others in your area, so if they can't help you, they may be able to help you find someone who can.

If you haven't done so, find out if you qualify for unemployment compensation. To contact the unemployment office nearest you, look in the phone book under job services, your state's department of labor and unemployment, or the state economic development office.

Help is also available from a variety of federal, state, and local public-assistance programs and departments. Check the government pages in your phone book for the numbers and addresses for what or whom to contact. Some of the federal services you may be eligible for include food stamps (through the Department of Agriculture); the Job Training Partnership Act (JTPA), a program for lower-income people who need to retool their skills; Aid to Families with Dependent Children (AFDC); Senior Employment. Check into various state and local programs as well. When you visit any state or local agency, bring your social security card, pay receipts from your former job, and names and addresses of former employers.

If you're in debt and face a financial crisis, look for someone who can help you set up a workable budget and a long-range plan to get back on your feet. If you don't know someone who can do this, contact the Consumer Credit Counseling Service (check the Yellow Pages) or Christian Financial Concepts, an organization whose trained financial counselors will help you reorganize your finances—at no cost to you. Contact them at the following address to see if they have any trained counselors in your area: Christian Financial Concepts, 601 Broad Street SE, Gainesville, GA 30501, (404) 534-1000.

If you are considering filing for bankruptcy and are facing all the financial and emotional fallout of that, seek help from Turnaround Ministries, Inc., Box 697, Griffin, GA 30224, (404) 412-9059.

Social Support

If you do not feel your social needs are adequately met through your personal network of family and friends, find a support group. If you need additional help, explore other groups that offer support for problems that may surface during an employment crisis, such as codependency, alcoholism, compulsive spending, and the like. The advantage of these kinds of groups is anonymity, which you may want and need if you are struggling with problems besides the employment crisis.

Emotional Needs

If you are struggling with marriage or family problems, you can find various sources of help, often with fees on a sliding scale. Your church may have people who are trained to counsel or who can refer you to those who can help. Or look in the Yellow Pages under social-service agencies, mental-health services, or human-services organizations for counseling services. YMCA and YWCA organizations may also be able to refer you to marriage or family counselors.

If you or your spouse is displaying the signs of depression—inability to cope with even small tasks, hopelessness, and inability to function—seek professional help. Ask your pastor, physician, a social worker, or other mental-health professionals to refer you to a qualified psychiatrist or psychologist.

Researching Companies and Industries

All the experts tell you to research the company you want to work for. What you want from your research is a sense of the company's goals, structures, functions, problems, and future opportunities and developments so that eventually you can talk intelligently about how you can help solve that company's needs to the person who has the power to hire you. But where can you find that information?

The company itself. Call the public-relations or customer-service department and request print resources, like an annual report or recruiting information, about the company.

Talk to someone who works at the company. If you don't

know anyone personally, find someone who does know one of the company's employees. You might consult a directory such as the *National Trade and Professional Associations* directory (available at most libraries) for the appropriate professional organization. Then call to find out who of their members works for your targeted company. If all else fails, you can write or call people listed in the directory to set up a brief informational interview about the industry, if not a particular company.

Once you find an employee, ask questions to find out what he or she likes about the company, what the problems are, what it's like to work for the department you're interested in (if the person knows anything about that department), where the company seems to be growing most, what the company benefits are, and anything else that will help you approach that company.

Community resources. Your local chamber of commerce or your local library will also have many free resources. The reference librarian can help you find directories and "job bank" books. The periodical department may have periodicals relating to your trade, including those that may profile the company or industry you are interested in. Newspapers may have featured the company as well, in the business section. Ask the librarian for help in researching these resources.

Developing Job-search Skills

Find help in developing your job skills in several places: books, seminars, and career counseling.

Books. Your library will have many books about finding a job. Consult appendix B for a list of what I consider to be some of the best books. But of course new books are added nearly every month.

Seminars. Besides the job clubs and support groups mentioned in chapter 12, you may find job-search seminars in libraries, community colleges, employment agencies, and outplacement agencies. Check your local newspaper and the bulletin boards of your library or community center for announcements of such seminars.

Career counseling. Career counselors charge for their services. Some concentrate on career assessment—clarifying what people want to do—while others focus on the actual job-search process. Some charge a lump sum in advance for their program; others charge by the hour only. Caution: Richard Bolles' *What Color Is Your Parachute?* recommends using the latter; that way, if you find you aren't getting anything out of it, you can discontinue without losing as much money as you would if you had paid for the whole program. Bolles' book also gives comprehensive advice on how to find a competent counselor.

Vocational Guidance

Find help deciding what you want to do for a living from the following sources: books (see appendix B), community colleges, outplacement firms, support groups, and your alma mater. Two specific organizations are worth consulting.

- Career Pathways, a division of Christian Financial Concepts, provides education, testing, and feedback regarding vocational choices. Contact them at 601 Broad Street SE, Gainesville, GA 30501, (404) 534-1000.
- People Management, Inc. offers a comprehensive assessment tool called SIMA (System for Identifying Motivated Abilities). Contact them at 10 Station Street, Simsbury, CT 06070.

Further Training

If you are structurally unemployed and need retraining, you may qualify for a government-sponsored program of some sort. Check with your local government agency to see what they offer. Also community colleges often offer specific training. Some may even offer scholarships for people who have been displaced in their field and need retraining.

Help in Finding Where the Jobs Are

If your main need is linking up with the companies that have job openings, you have several options aside from your personal contacts. Recruiters and executive-search firms come to most people's minds first. Technology is also making new networking possibilities every day, by way of television, radio, and computer data bases. All of these try to match appropriate talent with appropriate openings.

Executive-search firms. Companies that have job openings pay executive search firms to find people with upper-level management experience. If you are an executive looking for work, contact a reputable firm and ask to meet with them. Remember, though, that executive recruiters work for the companies that hire them. They will be able to help you only if they happen to have an opening that matches your skills and background. They should be only one avenue in your job search.

Recruiters. Recruiters, on the other hand, don't specialize. If you are considering using the services of a recruiter, check first with someone who has been in human resources for a number of years. That person should be able to tell you which recruiters are reputable. If you do use a recruiter, make sure he or she promises not to send your résumé out before contacting you first. Human-resource experts advise you to make sure that only one of your résumés is sent to any one company. Therefore, if you work with more than one recruiter, be careful they don't all send your résumé to the same company. And, finally, make sure the agency doesn't sell its client list—which again could result in an employer seeing your résumé from more than one agency.

Media. Some radio and television programs list job openings. One Baltimore radio station, WHLP-AM, devotes its entire format to advertisements of job openings and short programs dealing with topics such as how to dress for an interview, prepare a résumé, or start your own business. Call your local radio stations to see if they offer such services.

Also, at least one cable television station, CNBC, offers a program that features companies looking to fill professional and technical positions. Called Career Television Network, this program airs 5:00–6:00 A.M. (EST) each weekday morning and gives the viewer information on job listings, employment news, and career development. It features national, regional, and local employment opportunities. Viewers can call an 800 number to receive an information packet about any job mentioned, along with a questionnaire that they would fill out and return for a small fee (less than $10). The questionnaire results are then screened by the Cable TV Network by matching potential candidates against the profile of an ideal candidate the company specifies. The potential employer can then review these "electronic résumés" and contact candidates for an interview.

Like applying to a newspaper "want ad," applying to a job listing obtained through the media means that you are competing with thousands of other people who also hear about the position. However, you may be the best qualified for the job, so don't rule these out. Use them as a supplement to your work through personal contacts.

Computer data banks. Computerized job listings are springing up all over. Basically, information about your skills and background is fed into a computer data base. Employers tap into this base, search for people who meet the criteria for the available job opening, and then call potential candidates in for an interview.

Many colleges and universities now offer this service to alumni. Ask your alumni office if this is available and if it is helpful for those with job experience as well as those looking for entry-level positions. Several national data banks also may be helpful. One such bank is kiNexus, which works with several hundred hiring managers to recruit for both entry-level and experienced positions. The cost to be in the data base with kiNexus is $30 per year or $50 if the candidate wants to register with confidentiality, to conceal his or her identity. KiNexus also has an on-line data service that is more interactive and interfaces with an electronic bulletin board to dialogue about what you are looking for. KiNexus can be reached at 1-800-828-0422 or (312) 335-0787.

If you're looking for opportuinites within a Christian organization, InterCristo is the placement network to contact. Call 1-800-426-1342 for more information and an application form. Or contact InterCristo at 19303 Fremont Avenue N., P.O. Box 33487, Seattle, WA 98733. Phone: (206) 546-7330.

Much Cause for Hope

As you can see, many resources are available to meet your needs. The help is out there; it's up to you to get it. I hope this book has helped you work through the emotional, spiritual, and psychological blocks that can keep you from reaching out for the help you need. I wish you peace and prosperity of the deepest, most enduring kind.

• Epilogue •

Encouragement from the Trenches

"I've never had to face what you're facing," a friend remarked to me once. "My husband has never been without a job. But I've always been secretly afraid about what would happen if we had to face long-term unemployment."

My friend's words made me realize that a certain strength develops when our fears move from the back burner of "what if?" to the kettle of our current problems. The years of struggle Gene and I experienced have given us something invaluable: the knowledge that we can make it through tough times. We no longer have to secretly wonder, "What if our worst fears come true—could we stand it? Could our marriage stand it?" Although other people have been through worse things than we have, the tough times we have known encourage us to believe that with God's help we can make it through. Clinging to faith, faithfulness, and each other, we can weather other terrible storms that may come our way. After all, look how much we have endured. Look how faithful God has been. Look at the resources that have been available just when we needed them.

Gene and I have learned some powerful lessons, lessons that serve as anchors for our souls, a compass for our path. The other couples who have shared their journeys in these pages have also learned important lessons. We hope these lessons will help you approach work and life in a wiser, more balanced way.

NOBODY CARES ABOUT YOUR CAREER AS MUCH AS YOU DO

Many men who thought they had a stable career because they worked for a good, prosperous company received a rude awakening in the era of downsizing, mergers, and acquisitions. They learned the hard way what some career experts urge all of us to believe: that nobody else really cares about your career as you do. You must take charge of your career, each step of the way. "Always have a Plan B," advise John Crystal and Richard Bolles.

Men who are burned by unemployment are likely to be very cautious, even when they are employed again. One man, who had been fired and then unemployed for almost two years, said that even after three years, he wasn't sure he was over it completely. This anxiety was common not only for the men but for the women as well. Once a man finds another job, no matter how good it is, he and his wife live with the fear that an employment crisis may happen again. And that's realistic; "last hired first fired" is still sometimes true. Leftover anxiety is common, and it can either hurt or help your career.

Anxiety can hurt you if you let it interfere with your performance on your new job. But it can help you if you use it to spur you to have that "Plan B"—just in case. Some experts even advise that your job search should not end just because you find another job, even if the new job is an outstanding one. The ability to keep your options open at all times reduces your anxiety over having lost a job and provides positive career-growth potential: your radar is always searching for what else is out there.

Unemployment will also make you more sensitive to changes in your new company's financial health. This can be a very useful defense mechanism. One of the most important lessons you can learn from having experienced a job loss is how to avoid it again in the future. Not only can you read the signs better than before, you are also more adept at finding a new job, should that skill ever be necessary again.

JOB CRISES CAN HELP YOU REALIZE YOUR DREAMS

For some men, a job crisis is just the spur they need to revive their dreams. Some go back to school; some start their own business; some become consultants; some change careers completely, finally doing what they always wanted to do with their lives.

Don Markham was laid off at age fifty-one. He had been a vice-president and general manager of a large transportation company that had been bought out. When he looked for a job at his age, he repeatedly heard those dreaded words: "You're overqualified." He began to look at his life and ask himself, "What do I enjoy doing?" The answer for him was writing and speaking. He was already doing it for free, but he had not practiced those skills in his job. He started looking into what industries needed people who could write and speak. He got involved in executive recruiting and outplacement work. "At age sixty-one I was offered a job I couldn't refuse," he said. "And I worked until I was sixty-eight and earned more money than I'd ever earned before.

"It sounds like Pollyanna," said Don, "but it's true: this can be an opportunity you may never have again. This may be the chance to do what you really like doing, and if you like doing it, you'll do it well. And if you do it well, people will pay you to do it."

JOB CRISES CAN PUT LIFE IN PERSPECTIVE

Many men discovered during an unemployment crisis just how little control they had over their own lives. One engineer recalled, "I was absolutely committed to my former employer. I routinely used to put in fourteen- or fifteen-hour days, and I can't count the number of weekends I lost. I'll never be that dedicated again. I look at my new job as strictly a business relationship. They pay me to do good work, and in exchange I give them good work and a reasonable work week. But they don't own my life, and they never will. I'm not as inclined to work late or be there on Saturday. When I was out of work, I realized how important my family and friends were in pulling me through. Now I realize that no job will ever again be important enough for me to sacrifice my family for the sake of the job."[1]

Another man who is underemployed and underpaid, working constantly to make ends meet and never seeing his family, is now making plans to move to a less expensive area of the country and finish his doctoral degree. Men are discovering that having a good job isn't the only prerequisite for a satisfying life. They are rediscovering their spouses, their families, their friends, their interests . . . their life.

JOB CRISES CAN BUILD STRONG RELATIONSHIPS

Career trauma has a way of sifting your relationships so that only the good friends are left. And a job crisis tests the strength of your marriage. As you and your spouse walk through the fire of uncertainty, tension, self-doubt, anxiety, and waiting, the impurities are refined away, and you emerge as gold or silver.

For those of you who are still in the fire: persevere. Don't give up on yourself or your spouse. If you see things in yourself you can change, work on those things. If you need to let your spouse know how to help, express your needs. Don't give up. As Bob Marone said, "Now I know that Kerry loves me. She has stuck by me through this hell and has not given up." Norma Lorner related that her marriage was more solid than ever: "Tom has seen me at my worst and still loves me."

JOB CRISES TEACH FINANCIAL LESSONS

Some of the more painful—and valuable—lessons from an employment crisis are financial. Families who had been in debt, some of whom ended up declaring bankruptcy, discovered just how destructive consumer debt can be. Said one man, "If I learned nothing else from being out of work, it's that credit cards can eat you alive if you let them." People have had to cut up their credit cards to keep from using them because this society so readily solves its financial problems with plastic.

People learned that they could live on far less than they thought possible before the crisis. They learned just how resourceful they could be. They learned the humbling lessons of being on the receiving end of the grace of others. Those who have seen the other side of their crises have not forgotten the needs of others. Vic and Betsey Glavach kept a list of all the gifts they received so they could pay them back as they're able. If someone doesn't want to be paid back, the Glavaches will use the money to do the same thing for someone else in need.

Pam Grisweiler admitted that in retrospect she was glad they went through Mitch's unemployment. "We learned to live simply. We had grown up affluent. Now that we're financially secure, we still live simply, by choice." Mitch added, "Living simply allows us to contribute more to those who do need assistance."

Savings take on a new meaning because of a job crisis. I

know I get extremely nervous if our four- to six-month cash reserve gets too low; I am all too aware of how quickly a job crisis, or an unexpected medical or household expense, can eat into those savings.

Yet, even as Gene and I try to be more in control of our own careers and finances, we are ever aware of how dependent we are on God. The spiritual lessons are perhaps the most important of all.

JOB CRISES TEACH LESSONS IN HUMILITY AND DEPENDENCE

Career trauma marks a person for life. As Martha Catlin said, "It's like having a heart attack; you never again take things lightly. You realize just how tenuous life is."

With this realization comes a profound sense of dependence on God—at least for Gene and me. We have learned that all the things this world trains us to look to for our value—status, financial security, even something useful to do—these things do not give us one milligram of value. God alone gives each of us value.

Dr. Verle Bell, a psychologist with the Minirth Meier Clinic, speaks of three kinds of value God grants us: "just because value," "design value," and "tool value." "Just because value" means God loves us just because he has chosen to do so; his love is not dependent on us in the least. "Design value" is the value God has given us because of the way he designed us; we are each unique expressions of his creativity and goodness. Finally, "tool value" means that he has decided that we can be useful to him as we yield ourselves, our time, our talents, and our energy to doing his will.

Though the struggle has been difficult for Gene, it has taught him much about God's grace. "People who are successful and don't seem to have any problems have a hard time seeing themselves as messed up in some essential way," he said. In other words, they have a hard time seeing themselves as sinners in need of God. "What they miss," Gene said, "is seeing how big God is."

I can also see that Gene's experiences have deepened the very gifts he's been given—gifts that enable him to empathize with the struggles of others. He believes his experiences have sensitized him to the pain of others, not just people he knows but strangers as well. "A social conscience is a good thing to have," he told me. "I would hate to be a person who didn't weep about the tragedy in Somalia or the victims of a natural disaster." He's also able to feel a kinship with those who feel disenfranchised, because "being underemployed in a culture that's desperate for achievers" thrusts one on the outside of the mainstream.

Neither Gene nor I know exactly how God will use these experiences in the future. But we cling to the hope that the hard times were not punishment but preparation for some good thing God has in mind. It seems he has been pruning Gene and me, as he has pruned so many others who have shared their stories here.

I will end by sharing this story written by Kay Marshall Strom, whose husband went through eleven months of unemployment. To me, her words express a beautiful parable of what can come of a career crisis—or any crisis.[2]

Kay's Peach Tree

"A peach tree stands in our backyard. Unpruned, the tree grew big and leafy. And it was loaded with peaches, although the fruit was disappointingly small and tasteless.

"The year he was out of work, Larry went to work on the tree. When I came home from school one day and saw how far back he had pruned it, I stared in shock. 'You've killed it,' I cried. 'Now we won't have any peaches at all.'

"I was wrong. That spring the pruned branches burst

forth with a beautiful blanketing of pink blossoms. Soon little green peaches replaced the blossoms. 'Leave them alone,' I begged. Larry ignored me and thinned the fruit.

"By the end of summer the branches were so heavily laden with fruit they had to be propped up. And the peaches—oh, how large and sweet and juicy they were. There was no denying it: the tree was far better off for the painful cutting it endured under Larry's pruning shears.

"No one wants to go through troubles and suffering and pain. But looking back, Larry and I can only say, 'Thank you, Lord, for pruning us. Thank you for teaching us to trust you. Thank you for drawing us together as a family and welding us in a way that never happened in happier times. Thank you, that after seeing each other at our worst, we still want to be together.'"

• Appendix A •

How to Find Your Motivated Abilities and Skills

Self-assessment—knowing what kind of work you enjoy doing and do well—is an important part of job satisfaction. A career crisis may be just the impetus to spur you to discovering what you really want to accomplish in life. That may mean a career change, or it may mean a new direction, building on your past accomplishments. But knowing what intrinsically motivates you is the foundation for a lifetime of satisfying work. How you express your motivated abilities and skills (MAS) may change, because the workplace is ever changing. But once you know your basic MAS, or your "gifted passions" as Janis Long Harris calls them, you can then adapt them to the needs of the workplace.

Several books offer self-directed assessment exercises (see appendix B). What all of these require on your part is time and analytical ability. What is outlined here is one variation of an exercise that helps you identify some basic motivated skills and abilities. I encourage you to start with this. If this assessment does not give you as much information as you would like, or if you enjoy the process of narrating your accomplishments and analyzing them, you might want to check out some of the books mentioned in appendix B.

Step One: Identify Your Positive Experiences

Divide your lifetime in half (starting at age 5), and for each half list five to seven "positive experiences," as Richard Hagstrom calls them.* Here are the criteria for each positive experience:

- You did it because you wanted to do it, nobody forced you.
- It was a specific experience, like observing nature on nature walks rather than hiking in the woods.
- You enjoyed doing it.
- You felt you did it well, regardless if anyone else thought it was an achievement.

When you look for positive experiences, look beyond your work life as well. For some people who have never held jobs they truly enjoy, none of their positive experiences will be drawn from work. Think about experiences from leisure pursuits, education, home life, vacations, as well as work.

Step Two: Elaborate on Each Positive Experience

You will need to tell in more detail exactly what you did in each positive experience, how you did it, and what you found satisfying. If you enjoy writing, take one (or more) sheets of paper to detail each experience. If you would rather talk than write, ask someone to interview you and tape the interview. Whether you write or talk, be sure to answer the following questions for each experience:

- How did you initially become involved?
- Exactly *what* did you do?
- *How* did you do it? (details and examples)
- What was especially enjoyable or satisfying to you?

---

*Many people use the word "accomplishment" instead of "positive experience," but I prefer Hagstrom's term "positive experiences" because it is less intimidating.

If you choose the interview-tape format, instruct the interviewer to probe for clarification of any vague answers by asking for examples and illustrations. Ask "what" and "how" questions; "why" is irrelevant to this process and tends to mislead.

Step Three: Analyze Recurring Patterns

This step takes some analytical ability. If this isn't your strength, ask someone to help you. Look for recurring words that show the following:

1. What outcome you consistently sought (overcoming difficulties, completing projects, learning something new, building relationships).

2. The abilities you consistently used to achieve the outcome (teaching, writing, performing, selling, analyzing, helping). Hint: Look at the verbs used to describe the experiences.

3. The recurring subject matter (ideas, machines, money, a method, people, animals, tools). The nouns will tell you the subject matter.

4. The motivating circumstances (what animates you to your best work). Answers to the question, "How did you initially become involved?" may help you identify the circumstances that trigger you to do your best work, as well as adjectives and nouns used to describe the situation or experience.

5. How you like to work with others (team member, team leader, coordinator, director, manager, or coach). Note especially the prepositions ("with," "for," "together with," "under").

To discover your motivated pattern, write at the top of each of five pieces of paper one of these five categories:

- Outcome/results
- Abilities

- Subject matter
- Motivating circumstances
- Operating relationships

Go through what you said or wrote about each positive experience, and look for recurring words and phrases that fit in these five categories. Write them down on the appropriate sheet of paper.

When you are finished with this step, you will have clusters of recurring phrases for each of the five elements of your MAS pattern.

Congratulations! If you have done this exercise thoroughly, you will have a good picture of what you are motivated to do. Maybe this exercise has already confirmed what you knew, or maybe you found some answers to why a job has frustrated you.

Your MAS is the foundation for all the following steps of a thorough job search:

- Developing a résumé (Now you have the skills, evidence, and words to help you write one.)
- Researching possible industries and companies
- Networking for information, leads, and jobs
- Interviewing and even negotiating salary and benefits (You do know how good you are, don't you?)

God has created your unique design. He will also open and close doors according to his perfect and sometimes mysterious will.

Beyond Gifts: Define Your Mission

It will help you a great deal to take an extra step beyond identifying your MAS, to define on paper what you believe your life purpose is—the reason you have been put on this earth. A life-purpose statement will help you evaluate opportunities as they arise in all areas of life. You can measure each opportunity against how it will help you or hinder you from fulfilling what you feel God has called you to do.

A life-purpose statement takes into account not only your motivated abilities and skills but also your values and priorities. It should answer the question, "Given my unique set of experiences, gifts, desires, values, and aspirations, what was I put on this earth to accomplish?"

Your life purpose will undoubtedly include using the talent that gives you the most pleasure to use, the ability that makes you lose all track of time when you exercise it. In addition, it will also relate to your answer to the following questions.

- What kinds of needs, problems, and issues concern you most deeply? Look at your whole life, not just work.
- If you could do what you really wanted, what would you do? If you didn't have to earn money, what would you do to feel useful?

When thinking through these questions, make sure your answers reflect your desires and not what you think others would expect of you.

It's also helpful to separate your "be" purpose from your "do" purpose. The former is what you want to become in your character in order to accomplish your purpose. The "do" purpose expresses the means for accomplishing your purpose.

As an example, Gene has consented to sharing his life purpose. He learned, through the MAS, that some of his strongest gifts are "evaluating people's emotions, lifestyles, or needs; thinking through, planning for, and generally tailoring or devising; observing, perceiving, or assessing; being a proponent of, establishing a rapport, getting to know." His life purpose is to "listen to and understand people, especially their cultural thought and emotional makeup, communicating with them verbally about who they are and facilitating and enabling them to better themselves." His "be" purpose: to be an encourager for people, letting them know that God loves them as they are. How he does this (his "do" purpose) is through listening and helping people identify their needs and the ways they can go about meeting those needs. He relates to them as whole people, helping them to understand not only themselves but also the cultural, emotional, spiritual, and other factors that shape them.

Note that Gene can accomplish his life purpose in both personal and professional settings. A life purpose should be broad enough to apply to all areas of your life—as a spouse, parent, worker, friend, church and community member. It should reflect your "gifted passion" and your deepest values. If it does these things, it will serve as a very useful compass and a source of meaning in your life.

Questions About MAS

Many people have questions about discovering their MAS pattern. Let me answer a few commonly asked questions.

My job used skills that show up in some areas, but they aren't the skills that seem to be strongest. Does this mean I'm in the wrong career?

Career consultant Richard Hagstrom developed the Green Light Concept to help people determine the answer to this question. The green of the traffic light represents your MAS—those things you do well and enjoy doing. Green means go, full speed ahead. With training and experience, we can do our greens at A-level proficiency. Some elements of our pattern we do reasonably well—for a time. Hagstrom calls these yellows. You may enjoy doing something that's yellow—to a certain point. Doing your yellow more than 40 percent of the time, however, will turn it into a red; after a point you won't do it well and won't enjoy doing it. Red refers to things you do not enjoy doing, things you don't feel you do well. Hagstrom calls reds "limibilities."

Many people who burn out on their jobs are in jobs that are yellow for them. They wonder why they no longer feel motivated to continue. They may get fired at this point, or they may quit. They may feel disillusioned and confused. The answer for a person in this position would be to take some time to discover his or her green areas.

To answer the question directly, this person may or may not be in the wrong career. All jobs will include some green, yellow, and red areas. The key is in the proportion. A satisfying job would be at least 40 percent green (direct use of your MAS), 20–40 percent yellow, and no more than 20 percent red. If a job contains too much yellow and red and not enough green, a change might be necessary.

My MAS are all in things that I did outside the job. How can I convince an employer that I can do these things?

Much depends on what the positive experiences were. If they were achievements from a hobby, educational experiences, or volunteer work, you may be able to include those convincingly in a résumé and an interview. If they were childhood experiences or did not produce results that translate to the workplace, you may need to obtain some training or experience in the field you want to pursue.

Investigate what industries and jobs use the skills you've identified and start talking to people. Let them know what you've done with your self-assessment and what you are looking for. Ask what qualifications you would need to be employable. Then, go out and get your credentials if you need to. You might find, however, that mutual excitement and interest in a field, coupled by your obvious self-knowledge, will lead to opportunities that don't require further training.

Now that I know my MAS pattern, I've discovered I will probably need to change careers. But I don't know where to start. How do I know what careers will use my set of skills?

Several resources will help you match your pattern to existing jobs. You'll find these at most libraries.

Information about career and job alternatives:
- *Dictionary of Occupational Titles*
- *Encyclopedia of Careers and Vocational Guidance*
- *Guide for Occupational Exploration*
- *Occupational Outlook Handbook*
- *Occupational Outlook Quarterly*

Information about requirements for various industries can be found in these industrial directories:
- *Bernard Klein's Guide to American Directories*
- *Dun and Bradstreet's Middle Market Directory*
- *Dun and Bradstreet's Million Dollar Directory*
- *Encyclopedia of Business Information Services*
- *Standard and Poor's Industrial Index*
- *The Standard Periodical Directory*
- *Thomas' Register of American Manufacturers*

Don't overlook newspapers, directories of associations, government publications, and business publications that may contain information. Consult with the reference librarian for additional help.

Once you do some library research, you will be able to approach people in the field you're interested in pursuing. Nothing substitutes for personal contact with people who are doing what you think you might like to do.

I never really enjoyed any of my jobs all that much. I guess you could say I've been underemployed most of my life. I'm having trouble coming up with achievements to list.

Spend more time determining your MAS. Don't focus on the idea of "achievement." For many people, that's a block because of any number of past negative experiences and messages from others. Just go back and think through any positive experience that you did because you wanted to, that you enjoyed doing, and that you felt you did well. Start with when you were a child. It's uncanny how the seeds of a person's pattern can be found in those earliest experiences. (A friend of mine in her forties is just now beginning to do public speaking. One of her positive experiences was orating on the front porch to her little friends.) You need to get in touch with any and every positive experience you had, without censorship from your internal "judge" who whispers, "That's stupid" or "You call that an achievement?" Silence the inner critic and try to come up with at least five to seven experiences.

Then analyze them. It may help to ask another person to get involved, someone who loves you and builds you up. Once you've identified your pattern of motivated abilities and skills, you may have to practice the advice in the two preceding questions: research what kinds of careers use those skills, talk to people who are doing what you'd like to do, and get any training you may need.

I know what I love to do—fly airplanes. But the airline I worked for is now defunct, and other airlines are still laying people off. It really depresses me to think I may never be able to do again what I love doing most.

Technology is changing so fast that many others are in the same position: even though they enjoyed their jobs, marketplace conditions make it impossible (or nearly impossible) for them to find a job in their field.

I would still encourage you to do a MAS assessment. Flying airplanes will no doubt be at the top, but you will remember other positive experiences as well. If you dissect all your positive experiences, including flying, you may find that many of your motivated abilities and skills are transferable to other fields. You can then proceed to identify what those fields are, where you may need extra training, and what is necessary to make yourself employable.

Your greatest challenge may not be in finding another job. Your biggest challenge may be in properly mourning what you lost, while at the same time trying to find a job as an airline pilot and investigating other fields. The grieving is necessary, even though in fact you may find another job as an airline pilot.

The same thing would be true of an executive who may have to face the fact that he may never be a vice-president or CEO again. He must simultaneously grieve his losses, maintain hope that perhaps he may get another excellent job, and keep exploring every option.

This is no easy task. My hope is that this book will have helped all who face it to meet it with courage, faith, and hope.

• Appendix B •

Resources

UNEMPLOYMENT

Coleman, Lyman, and Marty Scales, eds. *Unemployed/Unfulfilled: Down But Not Out*. Littleton, Colo.: Serendipity House, 1990. A Bible-study guide for groups comprised of job seekers and those who want to reach out to them.

Erlandson, Douglas. *The Job Shuffle*. Chicago: Moody Press, 1992. The practical and emotional issues of unemployment, based largely on the author's personal experience.

Hosier, Helen K. *Suddenly Unemployed*. San Bernadino, Calif.: Here's Life Publishers, 1992. Focuses on surviving unemployment and getting a good job.

Leana, Carrie R., and Daniel C. Feldman. *Coping with Job Loss: How Individuals, Organizations, and Communities Respond to Layoffs*. New York: Macmillan, Inc., 1992. A scholarly treatment of unemployment and how people and communities do and should respond.

Leff, Walli F., and Marilyn G. Haft. *Time Without Work*. Boston: South End Press, 1983.

Maurer, Harry. *Not Working: An Oral History of the Unemployed*. New York: Holt, Rinehart and Winston, 1979.

Both of the preceding books take a Studs Terkel (*Working*) approach. The authors interviewed dozens of people of all ages and backgrounds on what it's like to be out of work, how they're making the most of not working, problems they face in society, and how they can know themselves through activities other than work.

Morin, William J., and James C. Cabrera. *Parting Company: How to Survive the Loss of a Job and Find Another One Successfully,* rev. ed. New York: Harcourt, Brace, Jovanovich, 1991. Discusses career options, from self-employment to consulting to active retirement.

Morton, Tom. *The Survivor's Guide to Unemployment.* Colorado Springs: Pinon Press, 1992. Deals with the practical issues of surviving unemployment.

Riehle, Kathleen A. *What Smart People Do When Losing Their Jobs.* New York: John Wiley & Sons, 1991. Practical guide, including information about how to negotiate the best severance.

SPIRITUAL PERSPECTIVES

Friesen, Garry, with J. Robin Maxson. *Decision Making and the Will of God.* Portland, Ore.: Multnomah Press, 1980. Help for anyone struggling to understand God's will.

Wagner, Maurice. *The Sensation of Being Somebody.* Grand Rapids: Zondervan, 1975. Christian psychologist asserts that we need a sense of belonging, worth, and competence, which come only from knowing God.

Wangerin, Walter, Jr. *Mourning into Dancing.* Grand Rapids: Zondervan, 1992. Spiritual perspective on loss of all kinds.

PERSPECTIVES ON WORK

Bolles, Richard. *The Three Boxes of Life and How to Get Out of Them.* Berkeley, Calif.: Ten Speed Press, 1978. Bolles helps readers integrate the "three boxes"—education, work, and recreation. Good perspective for those in an employment crisis.

Gale, Barry, and Linda Gale. *Stay or Leave? A Complete System for Deciding Whether to Remain at Your Job or Pack Your Traveling Bag*. New York: Harper & Row, 1989. Practical questions and tests to help you decide whether it's best to stay at your company or move on. Includes interviews of prominent people who share their stories of how they made this decision in their careers.

Harris, Janis Long. *Secrets of People Who Love Their Work*. Downers Grove, Ill.: InterVarsity Press, 1992. Based on interviews with people who love their work, Janis Long Harris explores how to discover one's "gifted passions" in work.

Sherman, Doug, and William Hendricks. *Your Work Matters to God*. Colorado Springs: NavPress, 1987. A biblical perspective on work.

Sinetar, Marsha. *Do What You Love, the Money Will Follow: Discovering Your Right Livelihood*. New York: Paulist Press, 1987. Sinetar helps readers find their "calling."

White, Jerry, and Mary White. *Your Job: Survival or Satisfaction? Christian Discipleship in a Secular Job*. Grand Rapids: Zondervan, 1977. Looks at work from a Christian perspective and discusses ways to find greater satisfaction no matter what the job is.

SELF-ASSESSMENT

Bradley, John, and Jay Carty. *Unlocking Your Sixth Suitcase*. Colorado Springs: NavPress, 1991.

Frahm, David J., and Paula Rinehart. *The Great Niche Hunt*. Colorado Springs: NavPress, 1991.

Miller, Arthur F., and Ralph T. Mattson. *The Truth About You*. Berkeley, Calif.: Ten Speed Press, 1989.

All three books provide a step-by-step process of discovering innate abilities and motivations. Authors relate this self-knowledge to the world of work. Any of the books is a good expansion of appendix A, which is based on their ideas.

Christian Financial Concepts Career Pathways Ministry offers an assessment tool. Contact them at: 601 Broad Street SE, Gainesville, GA 30501; (404) 534-1000.

DEVELOPING JOB-HUNTING SKILLS

Bolles, Richard. *What Color Is Your Parachute?* Berkeley, Calif.: Ten Speed Press, revised annually. The leading bestseller on finding a job, and my perennial favorite for its completeness, warm tone, and perspective. The 1993 version discusses recent changes in the job market and adapts Bolles' approach to those who want to change careers as well as choose a career. But earlier editions contain his Quick Job-Hunting Map (also available separately) and (since 1989) a very helpful section on finding your mission in life.

Bramlett, James. *How to Get a Job*. Grand Rapids: Zondervan, 1991. Helps you uncover your latent talent and build interview skills. Includes a listing of addresses of Christian organizations and businesses.

Ellis, Lee and Larry Burkett. *Your Career in Changing Times*. Chicago: Moody, 1993. Steering your career amid the changes in the workplace.

Germann, Richard, and Peter Arnold. *Bernard Haldane Associates' Job and Career Building*. Berkeley, Calif.: Ten Speed Press, 1980. For people who know what they want to do; gives specific details on how to find desired jobs. Especially helpful for executives. Adapted from Bernard Haldane Associates' well-known program.

Half, Robert. *How to Get a Better Job in This Crazy World*. New York: Crown Publishers, 1990. Emphasizes the necessity of learning and keeping on top of developments in your field and in the work world. Readable, humorous tone.

Irish, Richard K. *Go Hire Yourself an Employer,* rev. exp. ed. New York: Anchor Press/Doubleday, 1987. A practical book about finding what Irish calls a "judgment job"—one you do because you want to do it, one that uses your most enjoyable skills and addresses real needs.

Jackson, Tom. *Guerrilla Tactics in the New Job Market,* second ed. New York: Bantam Books, 1991. This popular book has been updated for the 1990s with some fresh insights and helpful advice.

Krannich, Ronald I. *Careering and Re-Careering for the 1990s,* second ed. Woodbridge, Va.: Unpact Publications, 1991. Thorough treatment of the current and future job market and the skills, attitudes, and approaches needed to survive in it. Krannich also co-authored other books on specific job-search skills: *Network Your Way to Job and Career Success, Dynamite Cover Letters and Other Great Job Search Letters, High Impact Résumés and Letters: How to Communicate Your Qualifications to Employers.*

LeCompte, Michelle, ed. *Job Hunter's Sourcebook: Where to Find Employment Leads and Other Job-Search Resources.* Detroit: Gale Research, Inc., 1990. Helps readers find sources of information and job leads for a wide range of occupations.

Lewis, Diane, with Joe Carroll. *The Insider's Guide to Finding the Right Job.* Nashville: Nelson, 1987. An upbeat, easy-to-read, encouraging look at job-finding techniques and at what qualities employers want.

Sher, Barbara. *Wishcraft: How to Get What You Really Want.* New York: Ballantine Books, 1983. Encouraging and inspirational.

Templeton, Mary Ellen. *Help! My Job Interview Is Tomorrow! How to Use the Library to Research an Employer.* New York: Schuman Publishers, Inc., 1991. University librarian helps readers uncover information about a prospective employer. Includes a bibliography of hundreds of business directories.

Wallach, Ellen J., and Peter Arnold. *The Job Search Companion: The Organizer for Job Seekers*. Boston: The Harvard Common Press, 1984. Includes lists of forms for keeping track of the various elements of a job search.

Wegman, Robert, and Robert Chapman. *The Right Place at the Right Time,* rev., updated. Berkeley, Calif.: Ten Speed Press, 1990. Richard Bolles says, "[The late Robert] Wegman . . . knew more about what was going on in the world of work than anyone else in the country." His insights live on, however, through this book and others.

Wegman, Robert, Robert Chapman, and Miriam Johnson. *Work in the New Economy: Career and Job Seeking into the 21st Century*. Indianapolis: JIST Work, 1989.

Yeager, Neil M. *The Career Doctor*. New York: John Wiley & Sons, Inc., 1991. Deals with 50 "ailments that can threaten your career"—to prevent, diagnose, and cure problems before they undermine a career.

FINANCIAL SURVIVAL

Dacyczyn, Amy. *The Tightwad Gazette*. New York: Villard Books, 1993. (This is also the name of a monthly newsletter, available for $12 per year's subscription, from Tightwad Gazette, RR1 Box 3570, Leeds, ME 04263.)

Hatton, Hap, and Laura Torbet. *Helpful Hints for Hard Times: How to Live It Up While Cutting Down*. New York: Facts on File Publications, 1983.

Hunt, Mary. *The Best of the Cheap-Skate Monthly*. New York: St. Martin's Press, 1993. Simple tips for living frugally, from the newsletter.

Leonard, Walter B., and the editors of Consumer Reports Books. *Money-Saving Tips for Good Times and Bad*. Yonkers, N.Y.: Consumer Reports Books, 1992.

ALTERNATIVE CAREERS

Edwards, Paul, and Sarah Edwards. *Working from Home*. Los Angeles: Jeremy P. Tarcher, Inc., 1990. Practical, comprehensive, and readable book about starting, maintaining, and succeeding at a home-based business.

Kamoroff, Bernard. *Small-Time Operator*. Laytonville, Calif.: Bell Springs Publishing. Rev., updated yearly. CPA writes practical workbook for building a business around your interests.

Karlson, David. *Consulting for Success: A Guide for Prospective Consultants*. Los Altos, Calif.: Crispt Publications, 1991. Workbook format, covers how to become an independent consultant and sell your skills on a contract basis.

Kern, Coralee Smith, and Tammara Hoffman Wolfgram. *How to Run Your Own Home Business*. Lincolnwood, Ill.: VGM Career Horizons, 1990. Practical book takes readers from deciding if they're suited to working at home, to selecting a business, setting it up, and keeping it going. Includes several worksheets.

Sheedy, Edna. *Start and Run a Profitable Home-Based Business*. Bellingham, Wash.: Self-Counsel Press, 1990.

OLDER JOB SEEKERS

Baker, Nancy C. *Act II: The Mid-Career Job Change and How to Make It*. New York: Vanguard Press, 1980.

Birsner, E. Patricia. *Mid-Career Job Hunting*, newly rev. ed. New York: Prentice Hall, 1991. Excellent guide for those over forty, especially executives and professionals.

Gross, Andrea. *Shifting Gears: Planning a New Strategy for Midlife*. New York: Crown Publishers, 1991. Helps readers consider major changes.

Kline, Linda, and Lloyd Seinstein. *Career Changing: The Worry-Free Guide*. New York: Little, Brown and Company,

1982. Helpful and encouraging workbook on finding new ways to transfer current skills.

FINDING A SUPPORT GROUP

The National Self-Help Clearinghouse maintains lists of support groups around the country and publishes a quarterly newsletter that monitors state and federal legislation affecting the jobless. For information, send an SASE to the National Self-Help Clearinghouse, 25 W. 43rd St., Room 620, New York, NY 10036. Indicate your interest in receiving the unemployment support-group list.

• Discussion Guide •

A career crisis can threaten you and your spouse in two significant ways: marital conflict and isolation. This discussion guide is designed to help couples or individuals in a group express their feelings and experiences and to learn positive ways of dealing with their emotions and situations.

Use this guide in a setting that best suits your needs. You may want to use it to spark discussion with your spouse. Or you may prefer to use it in a support group like the ones mentioned in chapter 12. You may even use the questions as a catalyst for keeping a journal or for one-on-one discussion with a supportive friend or family member. These questions are meant to help you process your feelings and experiences and formulate some strategies for coping with your unique situation.

You will gain the most from this discussion guide if you follow these guidelines:

Prepare. The questions are based on material presented in each chapter. If you do not read the chapter, you will not be able to respond authentically to the questions.

Risk total honesty. Whether you will use this guide individually, with your spouse, or with a group, be honest. The more honest you are, the more you will gain. There are no "right answers" or "proper responses." Let yourself own your experiences and feel your feelings. Only then can healing begin.

Develop accountability. As you commit yourself to trying various coping strategies, find someone to whom you can be held accountable, increasing your chances for success.

CHAPTER 1: Expectations and Losses

1. High expectations about career satisfaction can set up a husband (or his wife) for greater pain if he faces a career crisis. What is your expectation of "the normal career path a man is supposed to have"? Where do these expectations come from (your parents, society, yourself, your peers)? Do you believe men in particular have an innate need to be good providers?

2. William Farrell, a leading spokesperson for the "men's movement," says, "Rape feels to women like being fired feels to men." In what ways is this analogy true? In what ways have you or your spouse displayed symptoms of shame, powerlessness, and lack of identity since you became "vocationally naked"?

3. Many men experience a sense of "not being much in the eyes of others" when they don't have a good job. Has this been a struggle for you? In what situations or with which people do you tend to feel most uncomfortable?

4. Unemployment leads to many losses: loss of identity, loss of office, loss of connections, loss of control, loss of social contacts, loss of income, loss of faith in "The System." Which of these losses have you felt most keenly? Are you allowing yourself and your spouse to grieve these losses? If not, what feels most threatening?

CHAPTER 2: Emotions of a Job Crisis

1. The emotions of change—and any job crisis means change—parallel that of grief, with a few added twists. Where do you feel you are now in the grieving process

(shock, relief, denial, anger, guilt and inferiority, facing reality, depression and anxiety, acceptance)? What particular realities about your situation are you finding it especially difficult to face?

2. As you read over the steps to developing emotional resilience, which seemed the most challenging? Why? If possible, talk about that struggle with a trusted friend.

3. With the help of a trusted friend to whom you will be accountable, devise a coping strategy for developing emotional resilience, as suggested at the end of the chapter. Focus especially on those areas that are most difficult right now. For example, if you struggle with shame or isolation, concentrate on finding a supportive person or group.

CHAPTER 3: Wives Struggle Too

1. A husband's job crisis is also a crisis for his wife. *For the wife:* What feelings have you struggled with most? Have you been able to talk to your husband about your feelings? *For the husband:* How do you feel when you consider how your job crisis is affecting your wife?

2. What areas of your marriage have most been affected by this crisis? (Note: Husbands and wives should each answer this question for themselves, then discuss their answers together.) Examples mentioned in the chapter include invasion of a wife's "turf" when her husband is home all the time; tensions in roles; differing needs and styles in emotional closeness and distance; tensions over possible relocation; accountability to the wife; differing attitudes toward achievement; money.

3. What one thing do you wish your spouse could understand about what you're experiencing now?

CHAPTER 4: Marriage in Turmoil and Triumph

1. What coping strategies have you used to deal with the tensions in your marriage resulting from the job crisis? Which methods have been harmful? Pinpoint recurring negative patterns that you would like to change.
2. Discuss the feelings you find it hardest to express to your spouse. Discuss the feelings you find it most difficult to hear your spouse express.
3. Two issues crucial to surviving a job crisis are mutual respect and the twin tendencies of denial and isolation. Are these problems for you? How can you redefine respect (for yourself) and encourage your spouse to redefine respect? If you are moving toward isolation, discuss what you fear most in other people's reactions.
4. Go through the additional coping strategies mentioned at the end of the chapter and discuss which ones would most help your marriage at this time. Write down your goals and review them daily.

CHAPTER 5: Families Pulling Together

1. How has your current job situation affected your attitudes and actions toward your children (or toward the idea of having children)? What are you most anxious about?
2. What positive changes have you seen in your family? How can you turn some of the current negative aspects of your job crisis into positive ones?
3. If you have children, evaluate where they are in terms of their ages and temperaments. What needs or fears do they seem to be expressing? Try to see life through their eyes as you attempt to interpret their behavior. What steps can you take to meet those needs?

CHAPTER 6: Help Your Children Cope

1. What do you think is the role of a father toward his children? (Husbands and wives answer separately, then discuss with each other.) In what ways has this job crisis helped and/or hindered the ability to father in your situation?
2. Devise a plan for discussing the family situation in age-appropriate ways.
3. After reviewing the section "How to Survive—Even Thrive—as a Family," focus on several areas that you would like to improve in your family.

CHAPTER 7: What to Tell Other People

1. Who among your friends, family, and acquaintances do you most dread telling about your current employment situation? Why?
2. Discuss the hurtful responses you have received from others. What was hurtful? What kind of response had you hoped to receive? How have those relationships been affected?
3. Do you and your spouse agree about how open you wish to be about your situation? If not, discuss your differences. Look at the positives and negatives about your current approach to letting others in on your problems. What will be an acceptable level of openness for each of you?
4. Do you and your spouse each have someone else in whom you can trust and confide? Discuss with each other the importance of finding such support. Work out the limits of what you can and cannot say to others. (For example: "You may talk about your feelings about what's happening, but please promise me you won't blame me or bad-mouth me to your friends.")

5. After reading "Tear Down the Smoke Screen," agree with your spouse on which actions you will take to keep up a healthy social life.

CHAPTER 8: Recast the American Dream

1. What does the "American Dream" mean to you? Which dreams have you lost or do you fear losing?
2. What are some positive results of your situation? In what ways have your values changed?
3. What does money mean to you? What does it mean to your spouse? Discuss your perspectives and feelings with each other.
4. If you haven't done so, work up a budget with your spouse. Of the cost-cutting measures suggested in the chapter, which ones do you feel comfortable implementing? Which areas would you rather not compromise unless absolutely necessary? Discuss ways to cut costs and increase cash flow for your family.
5. Discuss the lessons you have learned so far from your experiences. Focusing on the positive and on the long-term solutions can bring a healthy perspective and a sense of purpose.

CHAPTER 9: God, Where Are You?

1. Do you agree that a job crisis is inevitably a spiritual crisis? Why or why not?
2. In what ways has your job crisis been a spiritual crisis for you? What questions have you asked of God? What emotions have you struggled with spiritually (feeling abandoned by God, anger with God, etc.)?
3. What illusions about the way life, God, or human beings work have been shattered for you? What one issue has caused you the most pain?

4. Where have you gone for answers to your questions? Are you satisfied with the results? Evaluate what has and has not worked for you.

5. This chapter suggests specific ways to gain new perspective on God, yourself, your situation. Which suggestions would you like to commit yourself to implementing in the next three weeks?

6. What specific things can you thank God for in the midst of your situation? Try praying with your spouse or your group about those things. Focusing on the positive ways God has sustained, provided for, and helped you will encourage you to see the larger picture.

CHAPTER 10: Help Yourself Move On

1. This chapter suggests a certain perspective as you attempt to find satisfying work: realize job hunting is hard work and treat it as seriously as any job; pursue at least one other interest or commitment totally outside the job search; develop realistic expectations; take charge of your career and learn about the rapidly changing world and workplace. Which of these attitudes comes easily to you? Which are more difficult to adopt? Which should you most work on now?

2. Rejection is a big part of any job search. How do you tend to react to rejection (avoid it at all costs; feel very depressed afterward; take it in stride; etc.)? What do you tend to tell yourself in the wake of rejection ("I'll never get a good job"; "They're right; I have nothing to offer"; "Better luck next time"; "I guess there wasn't a match"; etc.)? How can your loved ones help you better deal with rejection?

3. In which of the four stages of unemployment are you right now? What do you need from other people now? Have you asked those people for what you need?

4. After reading the nine-step plan of action, discuss which step you need to take now. On what resources can you draw?
5. Do you take time to reward yourself, to celebrate each small victory? Make a list of rewards you can work into your plan of action.

CHAPTER 11: Be a Supportive Spouse

1. In what ways have your attempts to be supportive to your spouse caused friction instead? What happened? Discuss your observations with your spouse and together discover ways to avoid the friction and give support in meaningful ways.
2. Is blame or control a problem for you? (If your husband feels blamed or controlled, it is a problem, even though you are not consciously trying to blame or control.) How can you practice forgiveness and faith so you can both move on?
3. Which ways of giving support come easily to you (defending, listening, providing a reality check, helping your husband feel needed and loved, encouraging)? Which are more difficult? Why? Choose one area to work on and set some daily goals. (For example: "Find one specific thing to encourage him about every day" or "Listen without interrupting during dinner time.")
4. What are you doing to take care of yourself during this crisis? Which areas have you neglected (physical, emotional, mental, social, spiritual)? Set a goal in each neglected area to help you achieve balance.

CHAPTERS 12 and 13: Support Groups and Community Resources

1. How do you feel about the idea of joining a support group? What image do you have in your mind?

2. Discuss exactly what you would look for in a support group. Make a list of possible sources for getting the support you need.
3. If you are thinking of starting a support group, discuss with your spouse or group some of the needs, resource people, and possible formats that might work in your community.
4. With your spouse or group, pinpoint specific needs and identify what resources can best help. Identify any road-blocks that get in the way of contacting those resources. Discuss this together and develop a plan to contact whatever resources will help you survive your crisis.

EPILOGUE: Encouragement from the Trenches

Make a list of the positive things that have come from your crisis so far. Look at each area of life: work, marriage, family, peers and community, relationship to God, financial concerns, personal character flaws smoothed out, etc. Then pray about your list, giving thanks together for all the evidences of God's hand in your life during this trial.

• Notes •

Introduction
1. Kathleen Boyes, "Man, Oh Man," *Chicago Tribune,* 14 July 1993.

Chapter 1: Expectations and Losses
1. Gershen Kaufman, *The Psychology of Shame* (New York: Springer Publishing Co., 1989), 35.
2. Jerry Cowle, "In the Crucible of Unemployment," *Chicago Tribune,* 17 February 1992.
3. Stephen Franklin, "Giving Up the Hunt: The Jobless Phantoms," *Chicago Tribune,* 15 November 1992.
4. Ibid.
5. Walli F. Leff and Marilyn G. Haft, *Time Without Work* (Boston: South End Press, 1983), 52.
6. Carrie R. Leana and Daniel C. Feldman, *Coping with Job Loss* (New York: Lexington Books, 1992), 46.

Chapter 2: Emotions of a Job Crisis
1. Carrie R. Leana and Daniel C. Feldman, *Coping with Job Loss* (New York: Lexington Books, 1992), 32.

Chapter 3: Wives Struggle Too
1. Gregg Lewis, "What Do I Do Now?," *Marriage Partnership* (Winter 1991): 26.
2. Maggie Mahar, "Trading Places," *Working Woman* (July 1992): 58.
3. Ibid.

Chapter 4: Marriage in Turmoil and Triumph

1. Loring Jones, "His Unemployment and Her Reaction: The Effect of Husbands' Unemployment on Wives," *Affilia* (Spring 1992): 61.
2. Gregg Lewis, "What Do I Do Now?," *Marriage Partnership* (Winter 1991): 27.
3. Ibid., 26.
4. Jones, 65.
5. Maggie Mahar, "Trading Places," *Working Woman* (July 1992): 61.
6. Lewis, 26.
7. Mahar, 61.
8. Lewis, 27.

Chapter 5: Families Pulling Together

1. Tom Morton, "Job Loss: How Your Family Can Thrive Anyway," *Parents of Teenagers* (January/February 1993): 19.
2. Tom Morton, *The Survivor's Guide to Unemployment* (Colorado Springs: Pinon Press, 1992), 128.
3. Ibid., 129.
4. Maggie Mahar, "Trading Places," *Working Woman* (July 1992): 61–71.
5. Jackie Alvarez, "Students and Trickle-down Stress," *Chicago Tribune*, 4 June 1992.

Chapter 6: Help Your Children Cope

1. Marian Henriquez Neudel, "A Flawed Image of Fatherhood," *Chicago Tribune*, 19 June 1992.
2 Kathleen A. Riehle, *What Smart People Do When Losing Their Jobs* (New York: John Wiley & Sons, 1991), 49–52.
3. Suggestions adapted from Kathleen A. Riehle, *What Smart People Do When Losing Their Jobs* (New York: John Wiley & Sons, 1991), 49–52, and Lynne S. Dumas, "Daddy Got Fired . . . Are We Going to Be Poor?" *Psychology Today* (March/April 1992): 32.
4. Morton, "Job Loss," 19.
5. Dumas, 32.

6. Ibid., 32–33.
7. Ibid., 32.
8. Kay Marshall Strom, "Fired!" *Marriage Partnership* (Spring 1988): 65–66.

Chapter 7: What to Tell Other People

1. James Hill, "Recession Strikes Fear in Some," *Chicago Tribune*, 27 March 1992.
2. Gershen Kaufman, *The Psychology of Shame* (New York: Springer Publishing Co., 1989), 45.
3. Kathleen A. Riehle, *What Smart People Do When Losing Their Jobs* (New York: John Wiley & Sons, 1991), xv.
4. Walli F. Leff and Marilyn G. Haft, *Time Without Work* (Boston: South End Press, 1983), 15.

Chapter 8: Recast the American Dream

1. Based on an interview in Susan Dentzer's, "The Vanishing Dream," *U.S. News & World Report* (April 22, 1991): 40. (Names changed to protect identities.)
2. Ibid.
3. Ibid., 39.
4. Richard N. Bolles, *The 1993 What Color Is Your Parachute?* (Berkeley, Calif.: Ten Speed Press), xii.
5. Tom Morton, *The Survivor's Guide to Unemployment* (Colorado Springs: Pinon Press, 1992), 82–83.
6. Kathleen A. Riehle, *What Smart People Do When Losing Their Jobs* (New York: John Wiley & Sons, 1991), xv.

Chapter 9: God, Where Are You?

1. Gregg Lewis, "What Do I Do Now?," *Marriage Partnership* (Winter 1991): 64.

Chapter 10: Help Yourself Move On

1. Elaine Gottlieb, "The Unemployment Boomers," *Chicago Tribune*, 2 April 1992.

2. Based on material from *Unemployed/Unfulfilled: Down But Not Out* (Littleton, Colorado: Serendipity House, 1990), 60–61. Adapted from Douglas H. Powell and Patricia Driscoll, "Middle Class Professionals Face Unemployment," *Society* 10, no. 2 (1973), and H. G. Kaufman, *Professionals—Search of Work* (New York: John Wiley & Sons, 1982).
3. See Janis Long Harris, *Secrets of People Who Love Their Work,* (Downers Grove, Ill.: InterVarsity Press, 1992).
4. Candace Walters, "The Advantages of Unemployment," *Family Life Today* (January 1981): 14.
5. Barbara J. Raasch, "Biggest Mistakes Taxpayers Make," *Bottom Line Personal* (February 13, 1993): 4.
6. See Richard Bolles, *What Color Is Your Parachute?* (Berkeley, Calif.: Ten Speed Press) for extensive guidelines for such resources. Among the best I've found are *Who's Hiring Who?* 12th edition, by Richard Lathrop; David Swanson's *The Résumé Solution: How to Write (and Use) a Résumé That Gets Results*; *The Perfect Résumé* by Tom Jackson.
7. Again, Richard Bolles has very good advice on checking out these resources.

Chapter 11: Be a Supportive Spouse

1. Gregg Lewis, "What Do I Do Now?" *Marriage Partnership* (Winter 1991): 27.
2. Ibid., 65.
3. Ibid.
4. Ibid.
5. Ibid.

Epilogue: Encouragement from the Trenches

1. Kathleen A. Riehle, *What Smart People Do When Losing Their Jobs* (New York: John Wiley & Sons, 1991), 172.
2. Kay Marshall Strom, "Fired!" *Marriage Partnership* (Spring 1988): 67.

• Index •